The Motivation to Work

THE MOTIVATION

New York · John Wiley & Sons, Inc.

TO WORK · Second Edition

FREDERICK HERZBERG ·

*Associate Professor
of Psychology
Western Reserve
University*

BERNARD MAUSNER ·

*Research Associate
Graduate School
of Public Health
University of Pittsburgh*

BARBARA BLOCH SNYDERMAN ·

London · Chapman & Hall, Limited

Library of Congress Catalog Card Number: 59-14119

Printed in the United States of America

58374

To Lewis Herzberg

Foreword

This book reports the findings from a study of job motivation based on a fresh approach to this problem. It is an important study, since the analyses and interpretations of the authors suggest that a breakthrough may well have been made to provide new insights into the nature and method of operation of job attitudes.

The senior authors were well prepared for their task, having recently completed a comprehensive review and analysis of the research in this field, reported in *Job Attitudes: Review of Research and Opinion.** This review of several thousand articles and books regarding the factors relating to job attitudes and the effect of job attitudes on work performance indicated much disagreement and confusion in the field. It appeared that one of the major contributors to this apparent diversity of results was the unstable nature of the subjective data on which studies in this field have been typically based.

Methodologically, the study presents a model that contains many aspects that might well be copied by future investigators. The authors have collected experiences, judgments, and observations by using principles of sampling, directed observations, and detailed reports. The data in each case included not only the specific attitudes in the job situation but the factors associated with these attitudes and also the effects of the job attitudes on work performance. The methods of content analysis were applied to the specific stories or sequences of either high or low morale periods of long or short duration. This study represents an important step toward increased objectivity, specificity, and efficient sampling of job situations. It represents thorough anal-

* Herzberg, F., B. Mausner, R. O. Peterson and Dora F. Capwell, Job Attitudes: Review of Research and Opinion. Pittsburgh: Psychological Services of Pittsburgh. 1957.

ysis of a large sample of systematically collected data regarding individual experiences.

There are few problems of more basic importance to our culture than an understanding of the motivation to work. As with all problems of psychology, there is an abundance of opinion on this subject, most of which reflects personal attitudes or limited experiences. Since the attempts at scientific investigation of job attitudes has led to such contradictory and qualified results, those who have strong opinions in this area become more convinced of the validity of their intuitions and biased experiences. These strongly entrenched opinions about the psychological nature of man cause many to discourage efforts toward scientific inquiry and to reject such studies when the conclusions are at odds with what has been previously believed. In this book the authors state findings and conclusions that are contrary to popular belief and at the same time highly critical of the attempts at worker motivation being made by the industrial relations departments of American industry. A careful reading, however, will convince the most sceptical of the soundness of the authors' arguments.

The presentation of this study in clear and simple language will be welcomed by company executives and others interested in this topic. Although the inclusion of much data is necessary to document the conclusions, they are presented in an orderly and logical manner and the authors move easily and admirably from the details to their broad interpretations.

This book is strongly recommended for the interesting and potentially very important hypotheses that it presents in regard to the nature of job motivation and its effects. These ideas should be immediately helpful to supervisors and managers. The book should be of valuable assistance to persons planning research relating organizational policies and procedures to morale and productivity.

JOHN C. FLANAGAN
DIRECTOR OF RESEARCH
AMERICAN INSTITUTE FOR RESEARCH

Preface

Why study job attitudes? During the period when the study reported in this volume was conducted the answer seemed obvious. There was full employment, with nearly 100 per cent utilization of plant and facilities. It was questionable whether the utilization of manpower was as complete. Thus industry seemed to face a situation in which one of the crucial ways to expand productivity was to increase the efficiency of the individual at the job. On the other side of the same coin, there was the continuing dread of the mechanization of people as well as of jobs. There was the feeling that in a world in which there was a surfeit of material things man was losing zest for work, that man and his work had become distant and alienated. Thus, both from the point of view of industry and the point of view of the individual, it seemed overwhelmingly necessary to tackle the problem of job attitudes. Let us be precise. To industry, the payoff for a study of job attitudes would be in increased productivity, decreased turnover, decreased absenteeism, and smoother working relations. To the community, it might mean a decreased bill for psychological casualties and an increase in the over-all productive capacity of our industrial plant and in the proper utilization of human resources. To the individual, an understanding of the forces that lead to improved morale would bring greater happiness and greater self-realization.

This is indeed a rosy prospect. There is no doubt that the large volume of research in this field, reported on in our previous book *Job Attitudes: Survey of Research and Opinion* (23), indicates that this prospect was viewed very seriously by a great many people.

At the time of present writing the world has changed some-

ix

what. Our economy is so variable that it would be foolish to predict its state when this volume reaches the public, but right now we are faced by significant unemployment, by an under-utilization of our industrial plant, and by a shift of interest from the problems of boredom and a surfeit of material things to a concern for the serious social problems of unemployment and industrial crisis. Yet the problem of people's relationships with their work continues to be a basic one. We should not overlook the fact that although the ebb and flow of our economy would produce occasional periods both of over and of under employment the problem of an individual's attitudes towards his job remains constant. For each man who sits at a desk or stands at a bench, no matter whether unemployment is rife or whether jobs are plentiful, the day and the task are completely different if feelings about the job are good or if they are bad. For any industrial concern, no matter whether its capacity is being used to 50 or 100 per cent, the attitude of its employees towards their work may very well determine success or failure. In fact, it may be that during hard times the edge that will determine whether a concern will survive will be given by the level of morale within the personnel.

A note is necessary on the ethical justification of this work. In a world in which organization men and hidden persuaders are fair game for every social critic the behavioral scientist who embarks on an investigation of people's attitudes toward their jobs must necessarily feel a trifle defensive. A noted social scientist, Peter Drucker, in addressing a symposium at the American Psychological Association, stated that an investigation of workers' job attitudes was immoral and unjustified. He felt that it was no business of anyone but the worker himself how he felt about his job. Similar feelings have been echoed by many others.

At the start of the research program the issue of ethical justification was raised and settled to our own satisfaction. The assumption was made that the best justification for this work was in its potential social usefulness. Although the danger that discoveries about the determinants of job attitudes could be used as a device for the manipulation of people was obvious, it was also obvious that men of ill will already had a plentitude of techniques for manipulating people. The kind of research to be done, however, posed the greater possibility that men of good will would be able to structure the world so that most of us would be able to live better and more fruitful lives. To discover and then reinforce the kinds of things that make people happier—to discover and then diminish the kinds of things that make people unhappy—is indeed a worthy end. No scientist in this age can ignore the potential for harm in his work. Neither can he be held back from his investigations for fear of possible misuse of his findings.

Support for this study came from a grant from the Buhl Foundation, along with matching funds from a number of industrial concerns in the Pittsburgh area. The following industrial leaders were instrumental in obtaining our financial support: Mr. Arch Murray, President of Scaife Corporation; Mr. Otis McCreery, Director of Personnel Relations, Aluminum Company of America; Mr. Louis Vayda, President of Bachrach Instrument Company; Mr. George Flaccus, Vice President, Jones and Laughlin Steel Corporation; Mr. R. P. Brown, Director of Industrial Relations, Mesta Machine Company; Mr. George Scott, Director of Personnel, Gulf Oil Corporation. In addition to giving their help in promoting financial support, these people provided important encouragement and facilities for our work.

Many individuals contributed to the progress of this research. Richard O. Peterson and Shirley Moscov Stark were of great assistance during the formulation of the design for this project and the execution of the pilot studies. We were extremely fortunate to have Alfred E. Pierce on our staff during a large part of the project. He carried out a majority of the interviews and was of inestimable assistance in the design of the analytical procedure for this study. Audrey Mayer assisted in the analysis of the data. Diana Fitzgerald and Gillian Whalen worked on the statistical treatment of the data. Whatever degree of clarity this manuscript has achieved we owe to Judith Mausner. Frederick Herzberg was Research Director, Bernard Mausner, Research Psychologist, and Barbara Synderman, Research Associate at the Psychological Service of Pittsburgh at the time the data for this study was obtained.

Lastly, we owe a considerable debt to the companies within which we carried out this study. They were generous not only with facilities for interviewing but also with the time of their employees.   And the willingness of over 200 of these employees to work with us during the progress of the research was the most important single factor in determining our success.

FREDERICK HERZBERG
BERNARD MAUSNER
BARBARA BLOCH SNYDERMAN

Cleveland, Ohio
July 1959

Contents

The Motivation to Work

PART I · Background and Procedure

Chapter 1   Origins of the Study

This is a book about people at work. More precisely, it is
about their attitudes toward their jobs. Work is one of the most
absorbing things men can think and talk about. It fills the
greater part of the waking day for most of us. For the fortunate it is the source of great satisfactions; for many others it is
the cause of grief.

People talk about work in many ways. Men who work together spin shop talk interminably. Sometimes this is idle gos-
sip about personalities and conditions. "Jim can't handle his
promotion, and if he doesn't watch out he will skid all the way."
"Sam is the man to go to if you want to get around all the red
tape." "The air conditioning didn't work today; it was hot as
blazes." "They better pay some attention to safety around here
or before long someone is going to get killed."

Sometimes it is the rich interchange of experiences and the
examination of problems of mutual concern. How do you work
for a man who can't delegate? How can we cut down on absenteeism when the work force is made up of women secondary-
wage earners? Do you really think they are going to put in
automatic controls and knock out all the jobs on the line?

When people who know each other well and see each other
often talk about their work, feelings about the job as a whole
come out tangentially. We don't have to tell our friends whether
we are happy or unhappy; the nature of our feelings emerges
from the welter of details. It can be inferred from the com-
posite picture of anecdotes, passing comments, and feeling tones.

The straightforward question "How do you like your job?"
is asked directly when old friends meet after long separation.
Then people stop and weigh the circumstances, the demands of

candor, and the need to add pluses and minuses to arrive at a total assessment. One man might say,

> Yes, on the whole I like what I'm doing. Teaching school isn't a bad way of making a living, if you call it a living. I like the excitement of watching the kids grow; at least, the ones that do. I like knowing what I'll be doing fifteen years from now, although I gripe about how little I will be making.

Another might say,

> I manage. The work is easy; the men I work with are a nice bunch. I'm not getting anywhere, but at least I have twelve years of seniority, and last year when production went down to 65 per cent they let thirty-five men go in my department but kept me on. I used to think there wasn't anything to living if you couldn't believe that someday you would make something of yourself. Not now. I get my kicks out of my boat.

Or worse yet,

> I feel stifled. The section head is always looking over my shoulder. I can't turn around but he is picking faults. I had five drawings rejected last month, and I know other men get by with a lot less. It's this recession and I can't move now. But when things pick up I'll be out in no time flat. Meanwhile, I don't knock myself out. I do an adequate job, but you can't put your heart in it when you know you're just waiting for a chance to leave.

It is the wife, however, who gets filled in on the details of these general assessments of job attitudes. She hears about what happened at the office.

> I was making a vital long distance call, even though it was against regulations. The division is woefully understaffed and I made the call in a desperate effort to get caught up on the work. My boss caught me and ripped the phone right out of my hand. I was provoked to the point at which I had to walk away. All day I found it hard to concentrate; my blood pressure is up and I'm so jumpy. First chance I get I'm leaving.

Or more chronically,

> I've been assigned nothing but tables and side arms to design since I showed that I can do these satisfactorily. I have no chance to show what I can really do and have no opportunities to learn. I'm nothing more than a number to the company which takes me for granted. My work has become sloppy and change slips are coming in.

A more fortunate wife finds her husband returning home after a day's sick leave looking better than she has seen him look for years.

> You know the company is making heavy layoffs now. When I came in this morning the chief engineer asked me if I had been looking for another job while I was out. He said, "Don't ever go looking for a job; I'll lay every man off before I let you go. You handle five times as much as any other man in this department." I hated to leave the office today.

This is the raw material of experience, the stuff of job attitudes. The scientist who wishes to study people's feelings about their work has to do more than collect experiences. His investigation must focus on specific questions. Three simple questions are implicit in the stories with which we opened this chapter. The first of these is how can you specify the attitude of any individual toward his job? The second is, what leads to these attitudes? The third is, what are the consequences of these attitudes?

An essential preliminary to a fresh approach to the study of job attitudes was detailed knowledge of what had been done and thought in this field. Fortunately, we had previously carried out an intensive survey, the results of which were available to us (23). This section attempts to summarize briefly only those aspects of the literature that are relevant to the design of the study we carried out. It also traces the steps that led to a formulation of the approach used in this study.

The Measurement of Job Attitudes

There is a great variety of measures of job attitudes. Basically, however, the identification of job attitudes has been done in three ways. In the first of these the worker is asked to express his "job satisfaction" directly by answering questions that investigate his over-all attitude toward his job, whether he likes or dislikes it. A good example is the work of Hoppock (25). The primary usefulness of this approach is in the investigation of demographic variables. Thus one can, in a simple way, compare the morale or job satisfaction of workers differing in age, sex, educational level, social class, occupational character, or position in a hierarchy.

It was apparent to many investigators that a worker could be asked not only to express his over-all attitude toward his job but also to evaluate his feelings about the many specific aspects of his work. Thus, in a second approach, scaled inventories of morale or job attitudes were considered. These inventories are predicated on the assumption that it is possible to summate many specific attitudinal responses and to arrive at an over-all score that expresses the worker's morale. The well-known inventory developed by Science Research Associates (53), which has been given in one form or another to many hundreds of thousands of workers, is an example of this method. As in the first approach, the scores on scaled inventories can be used for demographic studies. In addition, an analysis of the parts of such an inventory by various statistical techniques makes it possible to investigate the specific components of morale.

In the third approach no specific measure of morale is taken. A psychologist observes the behavior of workers. He infers attitudes, feelings, and motives from the behavior he observes. Typical of this approach is the classical Hawthorne study (51), which deals with the effects of group pressures of various forms and of supervisory behavior on the worker. There have been many succeeding investigations by social psychologists and industrial sociologists into group factors in industry. Like the Hawthorne study, they arrive at an evaluation of morale from the direct study of group behavior.

Factors in Job Attitudes

One of the major reasons for measuring morale is to answer the question, "What does the worker want from his job?" Answers to this question are important to industry in that they offer a clue to management in the never-ending hunt for ways of motivating workers. They are also of interest to the behavioral scientist in his study of environmental factors as causative agents in behavior. There are three distinct ways of developing these answers: (1) An a priori list of factors can be presented to workers, who are then asked to rank or rate these factors as to desirability. Examples are wages, supervision, company and management policies, and communication. (2) Workers can be asked to indicate spontaneously what they like or dislike about their jobs. An analysis of these comments would reveal the existence of some of the factors listed. Their relative importance can be deduced either from the frequency with which they are given by the workers or by some method of weighting the vigor of the like or dislike. (3) Multiple-item inventories or questionnaires may be administered. These make it possible to apply statistical techniques of analysis. From such an analysis it is possible to derive factors whose content can be deduced from a study of the interrelationships among the items. These factors have often been found to be essentially similar to those derived from the first two techniques.

As a result of an enormous amount of activity along the lines described, various lists of factors have been developed. These lists are basically similar but vary somewhat, depending on the source of the information and on the technique that was used to elicit it. In more subtle analyses it is often possible to do a demographic study of variations in the order of importance of various factors. Thus one can note differences in the kind of things desired from a job by company workers at higher or lower levels, older and younger workers, men or women. Unfortunately, the stability of these findings is relatively slight (23, Chapter 3). The one dramatic finding that emerged in our review of this literature was the fact that there was a difference in the primacy of factors, depending upon whether the investigator was looking for things the worker liked about his job or things he disliked. The concept that there were some factors that were "satisfiers" and others that were "dissatisfiers" was suggested by this finding. From it was derived one of the basic hypotheses of our own study.

Studies of the Effects of Job Attitudes

A demonstration of the relationship between measures of attitudes and resulting behavior is of the first importance. Industry wants to know whether the worker's attitude toward his job makes any difference in the way he works or in his willingness to stick with it. The behavioral scientist wants to know whether the measures of job attitudes have any predictive power. Unfortunately, it is difficult to evaluate the bulk of this research, since it consists of correlational studies in which comparison is made between groups of high or low morale, high or low productivity, or high or low turnover. There is a discussion of correlational studies at a later point in this chapter.

The conclusion from our survey of the literature of correlational studies was that there probably is some relationship between job attitudes and output or productivity. Unfortunately, the studies in which this relationship has been demonstrated are far from consistent. In fact, a well-known survey of the literature carried out independently of ours by Brayfield and Crockett (8) came to the firm conclusion that there is *no* relationship between job attitudes and performance on the job. The difference between their conclusion and ours was due to their greater scepticism of studies in which low, but positive, correlations were reported and to our citation of a number of studies with such low positive findings not included by them. Certainly there is no basic disagreement as to the tenuous nature of the relationship as it has been so far demonstrated. More uniform relationships between the worker's attitudes and absenteeism, turnover, and personal adjustment were evident in the literature we reviewed (23, Chapter 4).

Theory

The degree to which studies in job attitudes have been made a basis for fruitful theorizing is disappointing. We found relatively few places in which experimental or other investigations of people's attitudes toward their jobs had been integrated into the general body of psychology. There were even fewer in which psychological theory was used as a starting point for these investigations. Of course, there are some exceptions.

One of the most important is to be found in the pioneering work of Elton Mayo and his colleagues at the Harvard Business School. In one sense the famous Hawthorne studies (42, 51), carried out by this group, are not theoretically oriented at all. They call very little on the formal theoretical systems of any of the social sciences. In another sense, however, they are real contributions to theory. The discovery that the relationships between workers and their supervisors lead to a more potent influence on output than any manipulation of environmental conditions and that the informal associations of a group of men at work act as a potent stabilizer on the level of production (the notion of the informal group enforcing its notion of the "fair day's work") were made the basis of a new frame of reference in industry. To the extent to which this new approach, signified by the somewhat shopworn phrase "human relations," has led to fruitful research and to changes in industrial practice, this approach has fulfilled the function of theory.

The application of formal sociological and psychological theory to the analysis of people's attitudes toward their jobs has, as far as we can tell, been limited to the study of social groups. The theories of Kurt Lewin (35, 36) in psychology and of Malinowski (38), Hughes (27), and Homans (24), among others, in sociology have led to a thorough cultivation of the study of work groups. We refer in some detail to a number of these investigations at later occasions. At this point we should note that this body of work is only tangentially relevant to our own investigation. The studies that derive from it contain few direct approaches to people's attitudes. Typically, they focus on the *group* as the unit of investigation. The individual plays a role primarily in terms of his position in the structure of the group or his contribution to group processes.

Within this framework some useful concepts have been developed. First, a group can be viewed as having structure or form. This structure is dependent on the nature of communication among its members and also on the lines of influence or authority. An individual's attitudes toward his work can certainly be affected by his position within the structure of a group and by the nature of that structure itself (5). Secondly, a group can be considered as loosely or tightly pulled together. It can be demonstrated that the degree of attraction of its members to the group, its cohesiveness, can affect the group's ability to control the behavior of its members; this can lead to increased production when the group accepts production as its own goal and severely curtail production when it fails to do so (52). Third, a group has direction, and this direction is usually given by a leader (23, Chapter 5). The effect of variations in the nature of leadership on an individual's attitudes toward his work is far from clear. Although earlier studies led to the conclusion that "autocratic" leadership was inferior to "democratic" leadership in terms of the group's morale as well as productivity (29), later work seems to qualify this seriously. In one of the rare studies in which the nature of supervision in work groups was systematically varied, autocratic leadership seemed to lead to *improved* output, despite its deleterious effects on morale (46).

This current of research led to the notion that employees who are given the opportunity to play a role in the setting of goals and the making of decisions affecting their work will accept change more readily than those who are catapulted into change without any opportunity for the exercise of free choice (11). The notion of the value of "participation" is one that we utilize in the interpretation of our own findings.

One of the most important sets of concepts to be found in the body of literature on the industrial work group is that of "employee-centered supervision." Starting with the findings of the Hawthorne study, and taking strength from the conclusions of the research we have just cited, the idea has grown that a supervisor is successful to the degree to which he focuses on the needs of his subordinates as individuals rather than on the goals of production. In contrast to this point of view, which emerged from the Research Center for Group Dynamics and the Survey Research Center at the University of Michigan, we find a body of work that emphasizes the importance of the technical skills of the supervisor. Pfiffner and his co-workers at the University of Southern California (48) have carried out an extensive series of investigations in which they relate the organizational competence of supervisors to measures of productivity and turnover. The relationship of both to morale is not entirely clear, since direct measurement of morale is rarely carried out. However, there is indication in this work that a freer and more effective group will be found when the supervisor is given the authority to carry out his role and when he has a high degree of organizational competence. The importance of employee orientation is not denied; but it is clear that this orientation is not enough to produce a work group that functions maximally.

Argyris (4) approaches the world of industry from an entirely different point of view. Rather than concentrating on the group, he focuses on the individual. His contribution is a vigorous defense of the individual's integrity: the need of the person to maintain his self-esteem and his right to grow in the face of the demands of the organization for "teamwork." This attack on pressures to conformity is a healthy corrective to the groupcenteredness of much of the work of the Michigan and the California investigators.

In summary, we have noticed that the areas of study encompassed by "job attitudes" has certain well-defined characteristics. The measurement of job attitudes has been developed and applied extensively. Demographic studies showing variations in job attitudes among many different populations have been carried out. Factors affecting job attitudes have been identified, and their relative potential evaluated. Studies of the effects of job attitudes have been carried out, although the findings of these studies have been far from conclusive. Lastly, we have noticed the relative weakness of theoretical evaluations in this field.

A New Approach

A major failing of most previous work in job attitudes has been its fragmentary nature. Studies in which factors affecting a worker's attitude toward his job were intensively investigated rarely included any information as to the effects of these attitudes. Studies of effects, similarly, rarely included any data as to the origin of the attitudes. In most cases in which either factors or effects were studied there was inadequate information about the individuals concerned, their perceptions, their needs, their patterns of learning. The primary need that emerged was one for an investigation of job attitudes in toto, a study in which factors, attitudes, and effects would be investigated simultaneously. The basic concept was that the factors-attitudes-effects (F-A-E) complex needs study as a unit.

There are two possible approaches to the study of this complex. The first of these, the statistical or nomothetic, starts from the premise that it is possible to set up large groups that differ significantly with respect to some specific variable or group of variables. These groups can then be compared in an attempt to discover the relationship between these variables and various other measures. Thus groups differing in level of morale, high or low, can be compared to see whether there is a difference in productivity, or groups differing in productivity can be compared to see whether there are differences in morale. The rationale for this approach is that variations among individuals can be ironed out by the study of large groups. Our reasons for rejecting this approach are presented in a later section.

The second basic approach, the individual or idiographic, starts with the premise that the relationship among the components of the factors-attitudes-effects complex should be studied within individuals. That is, an attempt should be made to note, individual by individual, how given kinds of factors lead to high or low morale and the consequences of the morale state as indicated by various criterion measures. A likely way of doing this is to obtain from the individual an account of his periods of high or low morale. In getting these accounts we would be able to find out what goes on during those times that lead to higher or lower morale and what the reactions of the respondent are. Thus in analyzing the reports of such periods in an individual's life we would be able to delineate the factors-attitudes-effects complex. The strengths and weaknesses of this approach, too, are discussed subsequently. In the following sections we will say something about the sources that led to this approach, the basic design evolved, and some of the considerations that led us to reject alternate approaches.

Sources

1. Flanagan. Among the psychologists who have been using a technique somewhat similar to this second technique is Flanagan. For many years he has been collecting "critical incidents," among other things, as a basis for the development of job requirements (16). It appeared likely that many of Flanagan's critical incidents would resemble the kinds of accounts for which we were seeking. However, there is a basic difference between the two approaches. The goal of Flanagan's work is usually the evaluation of job performance or the development of a selection device. Thus the choice of critical incidents is based on a need to specify good or bad behavior on the job. These criteria are therefore external to the psychological processes of the individual reporting. In our approach the choice of incidents is based on the respondent's judgment of his psychological state during the events, an internal criterion. The criteria developed by Flanagan for the choice of critical incidents are not directly relevant to the uses of the present study.

2. Hersey. Implicit in the new approach was the notion that job attitudes varied for each individual from one period to another. One of the few people who had studied the variation of feelings about the job within the individual at different times was Hersey. In one of his best-known studies, for example, the cyclical nature of feelings about the job was related to the frequency of accidents (20). Workers kept a diary of their moods and records of accidents. The striking finding was that a large proportion of these accidents occurred during periods in which the worker reported his mood as "low." Here is evidence not only that people can identify their swings of mood and report on them systematically but that these swings can be linked to an important measure of effectiveness at work, that is, the occurrence of accidents.

3. Studies by sociologists and others of groups in flux. Work groups in industry have been dissected by sociologists and applied anthropologists for many years (3, 24, 58, 61). These studies include not only detailed observations of small groups, such as a single assembly line or a crew of machinists, but also, as in the work of Whyte, global views of the problems of an entire plant or even a giant company. The focus may be on the nature of informal structure and leadership in a work group and the effect of conflicts between the informal leader and the formal hierarchy. It may be on the operation of incentive systems. It may be on the causes for industrial strife. In all of these studies the qualitative, intuitive approach assumes the same frame of reference as our own. The factors that affect attitudes, the attitudes themselves, and the effects of these attitudes are studied as a unit. Certainly, these data can be used as a basis for inferences concerning the nature of motivation for work. In the third section of this book we draw upon several such studies (7, 56, 57) to supplement our own data. The studies of packing-house workers, steel workers, and workers in an automated plant observed by skilled investigators provide valuable material on which to test the conclusions derived from the results of our interviews.

4. The critical incident morale survey (22). The germ of our approach is to be found in the morale surveys in industrial firms, carried out by the senior author, in which individuals surveyed were asked not only to give statements about their morale but also to give examples of situations to illustrate their feelings. These examples, showing a high degree of specificity, led to some of the most utilizable data to be derived from the morale survey (21).

5. Content analysis. Data consisting of respondents' reports on events in their past is necessarily highly qualitative. We felt that some kind of quantification was necessary. Fortunately, the procedure of content analysis, as developed by students of political science and of public opinion, such as Lasswell (33) and Berelson (6), is available to translate qualitative material into quantitative terms. In a content analysis qualitative material is broken down by the assignment of individual ideas or thought units to categories. These categories can be made objective enough, by the development of concrete criteria, so that a high degree of reliability in their use can be obtained. The frequency of occurrence of individual categories can then provide a quantitative measure that can be used in precise tests of hypotheses. The possibility of using the technique of content analysis was one of the factors that assisted us in a choice of approach.

Elements of the Design

The design of this study emerged slowly through several stages. These stages are discussed in some detail in Chapter 2 on the pilot projects. However, at this point it would be worth-while to concentrate on some of the basic characteristics of this design, especially since they did not alter significantly from the inception of the study to its conclusion.

1. The specification of attitudes. The central characteristic of the design was the request made to the subject that he identify periods of time in his own history when his feelings about his job were unquestionably either higher or lower than usual. No attempt was made to measure morale or job attitudes in a more refined way. The advantage of this relatively crude procedure was that it avoided the problems inherent in the weighting of scores, the comparisons of the meaning of a given score from one individual to another, or the evaluation of reliability of measurement. One simple assumption had to be made. This was that people could place their own feelings about their jobs on a continuum, identify the extremes of this continuum, and choose those extreme situations to report to us. As it turned out, virtually none of our respondents had any difficulty in carrying out these directions.

2. The identification of factors in job attitudes. As we have indicated, the factors leading to job attitudes are usually measured by asking workers to rate or rank a listing of factors predetermined by the experimenters. A number of distorting forces can operate in such a procedure. First, a halo effect from irrelevant consideration in the testing situations can easily affect such a procedure. Second, when the person taking the test operates at the high conceptual level of ranking or rating factors such as wages, social relations, or supervision, the "social acceptance" of the factors would have an enormous influence on the rankings or ratings. Thus, if the person taking the test comes from a group in which it is impolite to value money highly, he would be unlikely to rank wages high even if this were of great importance in determining his morale. Similarly, the desire to please the investigator would probably affect these rankings or ratings. Third, it is possible that unconscious motives would affect the reporting of generalizations of this kind. For example, someone who was rather puritanical might possibly be reluctant to rank or rate highly the kinds of things that actually pleased him. A compulsive noncomplainer might conceivably upgrade all of his ratings, if a rating procedure were followed, rather than seem like a groucher.

We felt strongly that these distortions would be markedly less operative when a respondent was talking about actual events during a period of high or low morale, as contrasted with his ranking or rating general factors; that once he had committed himself to the choice of the period in his life his report would be less influenced by both conscious and unconscious biases.

In summary, the identification of factors was to depend neither on the a priori judgments of psychologists or managers nor on the generalizations of workers. It would be derived directly from analysis of the forces reported to affect morale during specific episodes in our respondents' lives.

3. The effects of job attitudes. As Wallace and Weitz pointed out in their article on industrial psychology in the *Annual Review of Psychology* for 1955 (1), criterion studies are the single weakest area in industrial psychology. Our own survey of the literature (23), as well as the analyses of Brayfield and Crockett (8), pointed up the weakness of the early work on effects of job attitudes. Productivity measures are always contaminated by external factors beyond the worker's control. These measures are often more important in determining his output than his own efforts. Indeed, for many levels within industry no objective productivity measures are possible. Criterion measures based on the ratings of supervisors or other observers are contaminated by all of the weakness inherent in the rating method. Even such quasi-objective measures as absenteeism and turnover are difficult to evaluate, since it is often not possible to separate the absenteeism or turnover due to external causes from that due to the worker's feelings.

Since so-called objective measures are subject to so many flaws, it was our feeling that the single best source as to his behavior during a period of good or bad attitudes toward his job would be the worker himself. If there exists a reasonable degree of self-insight and willingness to communicate, the worker himself can best tell whether his work suffered or benefited during the period he is describing, whether he was thinking about leaving his job because of his attitudes toward it, and whether his interactions with other people or his own adjustment were affected. Undoubtedly, many readers will raise questions about the verification of such reports on the consequences of job attitudes. The whole problem of the validity of these reports is discussed at length at the point in this book in which the data on effects are presented.

4. The semistructured interview. The interviewing technique used in our study is generally known as a "semistructured interview" (45). In this the interviewer raises previously specified questions but is free to pursue lines of inquiry suggested during the course of the interview. By contrast, in a structured interview the interviewer is restricted to the specific questions on his questionnaire; in a completely unstructured interview the ebb and flow of the interview is completely under the control of the respondent.

The use of a semistructured interview enabled us to fulfill certain requirements for the study. The respondent was given fair freedom to select the kinds of events he wanted to report to us. The questions were so designed that for each story we were sure to get the factors-attitudes-effects information for which we sought. The fact that this information would sometimes require a little digging was recognized in the instructions given to interviewers to use certain specified probes during the interview.

And so our technique emerged. We decided to ask people to tell us stories about times when they felt exceptionally good or bad about their jobs. We decided that from these stories we could discover the kinds of situations leading to negative or positive attitudes toward the job and the effects of these attitudes. Our thinking had progressed this far when a preliminary interview schedule was designed, and we went out into industry for our first pilot project.

Some Alternate Approaches

Although the basic outline of the study was set fairly early in the project, some attention was paid to other possible approaches to the study of job attitudes suggested by a survey of the literature and by our own thinking. It may be of interest to examine some of these approaches and to indicate briefly the reasons for rejecting them.

1. Scaled measures of attitudes and effects. The design that was finally worked out entailed the gathering of qualitative data about both attitudes and criterion measures. These data were then to be quantified by the application of content analysis. It was certainly conceivable that quantitative techniques might have been used directly in collecting the data. We did not want to use the most usual measures of morale because they are based on the psychometrics of a generation ago. Some of the flaws we saw in these psychometrics are discussed in the section on group studies. However, we could certainly have attempted to develop refined measures of job attitudes by using new techniques in attitude measurement such as those of Guttman [discussed in Green (18)], Coombs (12), or Lazarsfeld (34). The resulting information would have been more precise and more meaningful than that obtained by older techniques. Similarly, although there have been few attempts to construct new kinds of criterion measures, the work of Heron (19), who reported single over-all measures of "worker effectiveness," shows that they can be developed.

We felt strongly, however, that a qualitative investigation of the factor-attitude-effect complex was a prerequisite to quantification of both attitudes and criteria. Indeed, premature quantification might hinder investigation of the entire complex as an entity for each individual. Precise quantitative attitude measures inevitably are limited to rankings or ratings of generalizations, no matter how refined the procedures and items may be. The approach we chose was posited on the assumption that the best data for a fresh approach would come not from such manipulations of generalizations but from descriptions of events.

2. Group studies. The call has been issued in many quarters for an increase in the experimental character of work in the area of job attitudes. The chief technique used in the past has been the comparison of groups for which some known measurable characteristic can be compared as an independent variable. Thus the work of the Survey Research Center contrasts groups of high and low productivity and of high and low morale (30, 31, 39). In other studies groups that show higher or lower turnover are compared (32, 55, 60). Despite their real contribution to an understanding of the problem, these group studies showed some inadequacies. First, there was often considerable time lag between the measures of the independent variables which led to the formation of these groups and the various criterion measures which served as a dependent variable. Thus, an individual in a group labeled "high morale" at a given time may actually show very low morale at the moment at which he quits, has an accident, or slacks off work.

Another difficulty is involved in the kinds of measures that furnish the independent and dependent variables. These are almost always multi-unit measures in which the evidence of the weights of the various units is sparse. Therefore, an individual who shows a "high morale" score because of a fairly large number of agreements with positive statements about the job may actually show very low morale because one or two negative feelings bulk very large in his over-all attitude toward his work. A man who finds the work he does, his salary, and his opportunities for advancement excellent may have a high score on a morale test but may actually feel very negatively about the job if he is faced with an impossible conflict with his supervisor.

Presumably, improvements in technique could minimize both of these difficulties. However, even good measures of morale and criteria, if used to compare groups, give results of doubtful meaning. The factors leading to job attitudes and the effects of these attitudes have to be related to one another for each individual studied. In the end there is little predictive power to be obtained from a correlation between productivity of a group and its morale of +0.30, even when such a correlation is highly significant. The possible range of variation for any one individual is very great. The unity of relationships between antecedent conditions and resultant behavior is obscured by the confusions inherent in the design of this kind of study.

3. *Observational studies.* In an ideal world we would not only have been able to ask people about the times when they felt exceptionally good or bad about their jobs but also to go out and find people who felt exceptionally good or bad about their jobs and watch them over long periods. Although the report of the respondent would still be necessary data in that he would be his own best source as to the needs and motives which were operating, such observation, especially when carried out by more than one observer to obtain measures of reliability, would be of great value. Indeed, observational studies are at the core of much work in industrial sociology and social psychology as well as in studies in group behavior in other contexts (61).

Observational studies were impracticable for our project. There were neither the funds nor the facilities to engage in long-range observation. Actually, when the choice lies between intensive observation of a small group of people and the gathering of reports of their behavior from many individuals, it may be that the second course is often the better. Even the best observational studies are terribly handicapped by the smallness of their samples and by the limited amount of observation possible.

There is an additional hazard in the use of observation. Although the behavior of the interviewer undoubtedly affects the respondents' reports, it is likely that the observer, who remains in contact with the situation he is observing for a long period of time, exerts much more profound influences. The well-known Hawthorne effect is a case in point. No manipulation of working conditions or incentives affected productivity as much as the sheer exposure of the work group to observation. If it were possible to go into the world of industry surrounded by a portable one-way screen for observation and to carry out in addition a running interview with people to determine how they felt about what they were doing when they were doing it, observation would certainly be the procedure of choice. As it was, we chose the retrospective interview as offering the best chances for obtaining meaningful results.

Chapter 2   The Pilot Projects

The first pilot project was designed to test the feasibility of our approach. Three questions had to be answered. Would it be possible for people to tell us about times when they felt exceptionally good or bad about their jobs? Of more importance, would it be possible for us to develop from their reports a coherent picture of the factors responsible for their attitudes? Lastly, would these reports reveal the effects of job attitudes in sufficient detail so that a convincing account of these effects could be made? For the first attempt at data gathering an interview schedule was devised in which this was the basic item:

> Think of a time in the past when you felt especially good or bad about your job. It may have been on this job or any other. Can you think of such a high or low point in your feelings about your job? Please tell me about it.

In the remainder of the schedule probe questions were asked to determine whether information was lacking in the stories spontaneously told by the respondent: how long ago and under what circumstances the events took place; what had been the duration of the incident, and what were the effects of the feelings.

The sites for this pilot study were two companies, one a fabricating and warehouse steel company, the other a small tire manufacturing plant. Thirteen people were interviewed. These included laborers, clerical workers, foremen, plant engineers, and accountants.

All but one of our thirteen respondents were able to tell us about times when they felt extremely good or bad about their jobs. The exception was an illiterate unskilled worker with language difficulties. The stories were vivid, and, in most cases, showed evidences of deep emotion.

20

A first stab at the development of an analytical procedure led to clear-cut specification of the factors leading to the feelings about the job during the reported incidents and of the effects of these feelings. The sample was certainly too small for any conclusions or any testing of hypotheses, but it was notable that such factors as the intrinsic nature of the job, the characteristics of supervision, the relationships of the respondent to the social group in which he worked, the opportunity for advancement, and the characteristics of the company and management situation all played a role in determining the respondent's feelings about his job.

The effects mentioned were many and varied. There were specific references to the way in which job performance was affected by the worker's feelings. Several people told us about situations in which they considered leaving their jobs; a number reported times when their attitudes and feelings actually led them to quit. In many other instances there was clear indication that the worker's personal adjustment, his mental health, was affected by what was going on in his job.

Thus it was possible for us to state without hesitation that the technique worked insofar as it was able to give us analyzable data from which hypotheses concerning job attitudes could be tested.

An examination of these stories, however, revealed that our expectation that the data would consist entirely of reports analogous to critical incidents had to be seriously modified. Although several of the accounts did partake of the nature of critical incidents, in that they referred to specific, almost anecdotal situations in which a concrete experience was identified as being the focal point of exceptional feeling about the job for a very short period of time, in many cases there was no resemblance at all to a critical incident.

Here are some examples of the stories that fit the concept of "critical incident":

1. An engineering salesman tells about visiting a building in which materials on which he had "worked" were an integral part of the construction. It made him feel very good to see this because "I sweated out a lot of stuff working the thing out." This affected him because "it gives you new inspiration; I really had a feeling that I had a function, that I was an important part of the job."

2. A warehouse checker is ordered by his supervisor to go out in the rain and check a group of freight cars. He did not have a raincoat

at the time. In addition, he did not like the way the order was given. "I didn't like the way it was said. He did it wrong. You don't like the way things are said to you, you do things wrong. A lot of things come into your head." As a result, the cars were incorrectly checked, and the job had to be done over again.

In contrast are the following:

1. The same engineering salesman tells about his first job out of engineering school. He was hired as the assistant to a contractor and given the duties of keeping tabulation sheets and holding down the office when the boss was out. The boss was too busy to train him and seemed annoyed whenever the respondent asked questions. He felt frustrated because of his lack of function and because of his feeling that the job was a dead end. He was especially unhappy because most of the people with whom he associated off the job had interesting and vital occupations to talk about, whereas he had only the tedious details of his routine job to discuss.

2. An accounting supervisor felt wonderful during the period he was working on installing new IBM equipment. He felt especially good when it turned out after a period of time that the equipment was working, that the statements were going to come through on time, and that a real difference had been made in the functioning of his section.

3. An industrial engineer who was hired by a concern to develop a system of personnel relations and to reorganize the work of the concern felt very bad during the time of our interview because there was a strike going on at the plant and the management refused to permit him to handle the negotiations or even to sit in on them. He had the feeling that his own work had been responsible for many of the misunderstandings leading up to the strike and that he had the responsibility of doing something about it. He had been promised that he would play a very active role in the management of the company and that when the present senior managers who were near retirement age retired he would succeed to a high managerial position. His inability to participate in the negotiations over the strike led him to doubt whether this promise would be kept. He was, therefore, in the midst of a real period of low morale.

These are clearly not descriptions of specific incidents during which the worker felt good or bad about his job but accounts of longer periods of time during which the over-all feeling about the job was exceptionally good or exceptionally bad. They seemed notably useful for our investigation in that within them the factors-attitudes-effects unit could be clearly and dramatically described. Since these reports could not be called incidents, a new title had to be devised. The term "sequence of events" (which was often abridged to "sequence") * was applied to all reports given by the interviewees; a distinction between reports that were more analogous to incidents and those of the second group was worked out, but it was decided to gather both kinds of information.

The term, *short-range sequence of events,* was applied to anecdotal, narrowly delimited sets of events during which exceptional feelings were reported. These are most analogous to Flanagan's critical incidents, although, as we indicated in Chapter 1, the chief criteria for choice of an event to be discussed was the respondent's perception of a peak or valley in his feelings about his job.

On the basis of a preliminary examination of the stories we had been given in our pilots, the following criteria for a *long-range sequence of events* were designed. First, the long-range sequence of events should cover a minimum in time of several weeks to a month. The maximum could be any number of years. Second, the long-range sequence of events should be identified by the respondent as a period of time during which his over-all feelings about his job were consistently high or low, despite possible fluctuations of feeling or even minor inversions within these periods. For example, a worker who on the whole was quite unhappy in his job could occasionally achieve real feelings of satisfaction at the completion of an assignment or from a passing word of praise. This, however, does not minimize the fact that he could report a long period of time as being one in which his basic fundamental attitude toward the job was deep dissatisfaction. Third, the long-range sequence of events must be clearly bounded in time. The respondent must be able to describe the events that began the sequence, and those that terminated it, if it was not presently going on. This does not mean that the onset or the termination of a long-range sequence of events should be

* Since the writing of our book, a study with methods somewhat similar to ours has appeared. Caplow and McGee (10) in their ingenious dissection of the academic world took as the unit of their study each instance of turnover for a specified period of time in a group of eleven universities. They gathered all possible information about the circumstances relating to the departure of the previous incumbent and the hiring of his successor. This unit is also labeled a "sequence of events" in their work.

of necessity sudden or dramatic. However, in all cases the respondent must be talking about a period of time which had a beginning and an end.

The Second Pilot

The second pilot study was on a larger scale than the first. In this our intention was not only to develop the method further but also to do a preliminary test of several hypotheses that had been suggested by the survey of the literature and by the findings in the first pilot study. Also, in the second pilot a further decision was made concerning the population to be approached. On the basis of our experiences with the wide range of positions covered by the first group of people to whom we talked, we decided to work with middle management. This decision was based on two considerations. First, middle-management people are more verbal, better educated, and more conscious of the ebb and flow of their attitudes. They were able to communicate with us far better than the production-line workers or clerical workers to whom we spoke.

Another consideration, which was somewhat secondary but not completely absent from our thinking, was that industry was greatly concerned about the attitudes of middle-management people towards their jobs. We expected that our study would meet with more ready acceptance by industry if we worked with a group in which they were interested. Furthermore, the problems of obtaining access to this group would be minimal.

Thus the major purposes of the second pilot study were to develop further this method of studying job attitudes, to demonstrate that the technique would be acceptable to the people being interviewed and would produce material useful for testing specific hypotheses about job attitudes. Secondarily, the study was designed for a preliminary test of some rather general hypotheses:

1. Different kinds of factors will be found to lead to short-range and long-range sequences.

2. Different kinds of effects will result from the job attitudes shown during short-range and long-range sequences.

3. "High" sequences, that is, those revolving around good feel-

ings, will stem from different factors and will contain different effects than "low" sequences, those revolving around bad feelings.

The company in which we worked was an engineering and construction firm which carries on widely diversified projects. We interviewed thirty-nine middle-management personnel. As it happened, all but six of them were engineers of one kind or another. Some were actually serving other than engineering functions in the company but had an engineering background. The remainder were working as design engineers, project supervisors, or in specialized engineering capacities. Six men who had fiscal or administrative positions had no engineering training.

The reports they gave in answer to our questions were, as before, vivid and highly personal. We were told of high feelings related to exceptional accomplishments, both technical and in working with people. Low feelings occurred when the respondent received inconsistent answers to requests for a raise, for more diversified work, or for information about his future in the company. Here are some summaries of the interviews:

1. Before becoming actual manager of the department, I had nominal responsibility for a long time. I resented doing the work without having the position. I should have been called manager if I did his work; I should have gotten more money, too.

2. I was sent to the field with direct responsibility for three quarters of a million dollars worth of equipment on a fifteen-million-dollar project. The responsibility was great, and I proved my ability to handle it. It made me feel wonderful.

3. When I was a young man I designed a bridge which stands over one of the rivers around Pittsburgh. I got a tremendous feeling of satisfaction from seeing the bridge actually arise out of the plans I had drawn. I still feel wonderful every time I pass the bridge and point to it and say, "I built that."

4. I have a responsible position; I was told that the individual I replaced was not coming back. The former employee was told by the manager of the company that he could have his old job back at any time. The man I replaced returned and was given a parallel position in which neither of us was in authority over the other. Both of us found the position insupportable. I felt bad enough about this to quit. (We found later that he actually did resign from his job.)

5. I was promised a pay raise and it didn't come through one pay period after another for three pay periods. I was extremely unhappy even

when I received the pay raise because I felt that I should have been given the pay raise when it was promised or at least information about why it was not forthcoming.

6. I arranged a contract with a company to study a new process. It gave me opportunity for intensive study of work I and others had done in the past. We came up with a very attractive solution. As the work approached a climax I was happy, felt good. When you get it "there is no satisfaction like it."

The next step was the development of a procedure for the analysis of these data. Since the procedure for developing a content analysis was very similar to that finally followed in the major study, it will not be described in detail at this point.

The results of this pilot project were very encouraging. Virtually all of the respondents were able to give sequences of events that were analyzable. The analytical scheme, although it had certain real bugs that needed working out, was one with which we were able to derive theoretically meaningful findings from an examination even of the small number of stories reported in this pilot project. All of the people who were interviewed were asked about their reactions to the interview. Most respondents liked the interview; there were no negative reactions.

An examination of the analytic scheme and of the data itself revealed one glaring methodological flaw. The statements of respondents about what actually happened and about their psychological reactions to what happened had been indiscriminately lumped together. Thus a worker who talked about receiving a raise and the worker who said about a raise, "It meant that I was being appreciated," are really telling about two different things. In the first instance he was describing events; in the second he was telling us about the needs that were being fulfilled in the course of these events.

Recognition of this distinction led to two modifications of the technique. First, in developing the procedure for the final study from that used in the pilot, questions were added to insure that information relating to the psychological reactions to events during periods of high or low job attitudes emerged systematically rather than in a haphazard manner. This involved probes to determine why the respondent felt the way he did or what these events meant to the respondent. Second, in forecasting the nature of the analytical scheme for the data the factors leading to job attitudes were divided into two classes. *First-level factors* were to be described as *situations* that were antecedent to a person's attitude toward his job. Thus first-level factors always described concrete events or situations reported by the respondent. *Second-level factors* were to be described as the needs or drives activated by these events. The individual second-level factors would categorize the answers the respondent would give to probe questions about his reasons for feeling as he did.

In general, both in the conduct of the interview and in the subsequent analysis there emerged a new awareness that the inquiry into the factors relating to job attitudes had to proceed on both of these levels: reports on objective events and reports on the individual's psychological reaction to, and interpretation of, these events.

One further modification in the design of the study came from the discussion of the pilot. It had been previously assumed that no statements would have to be made concerning the intensity of the attitudes held toward the job during the sequence of events being reported. Nothing in the preliminary trials altered our basic rejection of the need for quantitative or scaled attitude measures. However, it soon became apparent that the events being reported varied considerably in degree of importance to the individual. Apart from the extent of the effects, some of the sequences of events were perceived as more critical to the individual than others.

Criticalness, we discovered, has many components. The questionnaire we finally developed attempted to attack several of these components. First, we asked whether the events had made an objective difference to the respondent's future career. Second, the respondent was asked whether his attitude toward any given individuals, toward his company, and toward his profession had been affected. The answers to these questions form the basis, in part, for later estimates of "attitudinal" effects. Last, a rating scale was developed. In this, the respondent was asked to indicate on a twenty-one point graphic scale how seriously his feelings were affected by the events. Both high and low sequences that were of great importance were localized at the upper end of the scale, events of average importance at the middle, and trivial events at the lower end. It was expected that the preponderance of sequences of events would be placed beyond the median position of the scale and that the bulk of long-range sequences would be closer to the top (more critical) end of the scale than the short-range sequences. Since many factors other than criticalness were expected to determine the occurrence of effects, we did not expect that either the frequency or the intensity of effects would be related to this rating.

Summary

Before the procedure of the major study is described in detail, it may be valuable to summarize briefly the modifications in the over-all design of the project introduced after the pilot studies had been evaluated. The central core of the design was the notion of the sequence of events as a unit, bounded in time, during which an individual's attitudes toward his job are characterized by himself as being exceptionally positive or exceptionally negative. From the respondent's report on this sequence of events the triad of factors-attitudes-effects can be studied as a unitary system within which functional relationships among the components can be described. These components were to be derived from answers to questions asked in the interview.

1. *First-level factors:* a description of the objective occurrences during the sequence of events, with especial emphasis on those identified by the respondent as being related to his attitudes. Example: a promotion.

2. *Second-level factors:* these categorize the reasons given by respondents for their feelings; they may be used as a basis for inferences about the drives or needs which are met or which fail to be met during the sequence of events. Example: a respondent's answer, "I felt good because the promotion meant I was being recognized."

3. *Effects:* the sole change was the introduction of probe questions searching into attitudinal effects beyond the behavioral level involved in productivity, turnover, or interpersonal relations. Specification of mental health effects was also attempted.

A further development was the distinction made between sequences of events involving many and complex happenings over a long period of time, the long-range sequences, and those which were unitary or incidentlike, the short-range sequences.

Last, measures of the criticalness of the sequence of events were introduced both as a gauge of the internal consistency of the technique (in comparing short-range and long-range sequences) and as a source of further information about the meaning of the data.

Little attention has been given to the hypotheses around which the study was built, since, to a great extent, the present study was more exploratory than it was hypothetico-deductive. That is, its major intent was to derive information concerning lawful relationships among the measurables, factors, and effects present in the design. However, certain basic hypotheses could be and were tested. These did, in fact, lead to the conclusions that are the substance of the book. The major hypothesis was that the factors leading to positive attitudes and those leading to negative attitudes would differ. A second basic hypothesis was that the factors and effects involved in long-range sequences of events would differ from those in short-range sequences.

Chapter 3

Procedure
for the Major Study

With a technique and a set of hypotheses to be tested, we were now ready to select sites and a population for a full-scale study. The choice of site was dictated by local conditions. Pittsburgh is a center for heavy industry, primarily the basic production and fabrication of metals. In addition, local industrial concerns design and construct machinery and carry out other engineering activities. All the companies within which we worked fit this pattern, with the exception of one, which is a major utility.

Specifically, these were the sites of the study:

1. A medium-sized company manufacturing special steels.

2. A large fabricating plant, employing several thousand people, that turns out consumer goods and material for the armed forces. This is a branch of a nation-wide metal company.

3. The central offices and plants of a major basic steel producer.

4. The staff of a concern that engages in a wide variety of engineering functions, including shipbuilding.

5. The accounting staff of a specialty steel firm.

6. The staff of a large engineering company that operates as a job shop for the building of heavy machinery.

7. A major utility that is part of a national holding company.

8. A small manufacturer of industrial instruments.

9. A small manufacturer of light industrial machinery.

It is readily apparent that these nine concerns vary widely in both size and nature of their activities. The characteristics of their locales are also diversified. Some of the plants are in the center of the city; some are in suburban areas; still others are in small towns far enough from Pittsburgh to have an essentially different social and economic milieu. The fact that this work was done within a thirty-mile radius around Pittsburgh will inevitably raise questions about the degree to which the findings are applicable in other areas of the country. Undoubtedly Pittsburgh, like all other urban centers, has some unique characteristics. Although we cannot prove that the unique nature of both time and place does not affect our findings, the setting for our study was, we feel, sufficiently representative of the urban industrial scene so that *some* generalizations from our findings are justified.

We interviewed a sizable group of people in each company. This might raise the hope that we could analyze the effect of a company's structure, personnel policies, or social atmosphere on job attitudes. Apart from the internal treatment of the individual sequences, this was not done. It was a central characteristic of our method in this study that the respondents were free to report on events in the recent or distant past, in their present or past places of employment. As a result, we would not have been able to get enough information about the state of affairs in any one company at any one time to develop an analysis based on the reports of many respondents working in the same setting.

Despite the fact that not all of the interview data pertained to current or near-current happenings, we did gain some insight into the existing operation of each plant as we worked in it. No attempt could be made to utilize this insight in the present work. The analysis of each sequence was based entirely on what the respondent told us in that sequence. The possibility exists, however, of a different kind of research design. The interviewing technique of the present study modified, so that respondents spoke only of the relatively recent past, could be combined with intensive description of the site. This would lead to a cross-sectional analysis of job attitudes in which an over-all view of the individual in his environment could be combined with an examination of the organizational units of that environment. These units could be work groups, departments, or even whole plants.

The Population Sample

In our first pilot study we talked with clerical and production workers as well as professional and managerial people. We discovered that the professional and managerial groups were more verbal, showed a quicker grasp of the technique, and gave more and better delineated sequences of events than the clerical and production groups.

The second pilot study was restricted to managerial and professional people. On the basis of our experiences in this work, we decided to concentrate in the major sample on engineers and accountants. It was apparent in the results of this second pilot that engineers were able to give exceptionally vivid accounts of their work experiences. Since our study was still in the nature of an exploratory project, it was vital to us that we mine where the metal was richest.

A sample limited to one profession would have yielded results of doubtful generality. To develop findings independent of the peculiar circumstances of the engineer, we needed to study a comparable group. Accountants were chosen because their jobs, like those of engineers, are rich in technique. This richness makes it likely that the accountant, like the engineer, would have much to tell us. However, the groups are vastly different in the nature of their training, their present degree of professionalization, the kind of work they do, and, presumably, the kind of people attracted into them. Last, by covering accountants and engineers, we examined the job attitudes of two of the most important staff groups in modern industry.

Our sights were set for approximately 200 interviews, since we felt that our resources would be adequate for such a project and that the amount of data we could derive from that number of interviews would be sufficient for an evaluation of the technique and for a test of the general hypotheses.

Sampling Procedures

There were two sampling problems to be solved. One was the representativeness of the group of respondents in the universe of engineers and accountants. The other was the representativeness of the sequences of events reported by these respondents in their lives. Unfortunately, it would have been difficult to describe the parameters of either of these universes. Therefore, a probability sampling procedure was virtually impossible.

The solution to the first sampling problem lay in an approach that insured a relatively representative cross section of both engineers and accountants insofar as they were represented in the segment of Pittsburgh industry in which we worked.

The solution to the second problem is less straightforward. We collected a group of reports of events freely chosen by our respondents from the totality of their accumulated experiences. This body of information represents sequences of events which *they* identified as being their own periods of exceptionally good or exceptionally bad feelings about their jobs. This is *not* a systematic sampling from the experiences of each individual. We could not institute any such system because of the inherent nature of our technique; the respondent *had* to be given freedom to choose.

Since there was no probability sampling procedure either for individuals or for sequences, it is important to describe as clearly as possible to the reader the way in which the individuals in the sample were chosen. Each company was approached for permission to work within it. After this permission had been obtained, a conference was held with some individual in the company who was familiar with the company's structure and personnel. We then presented this individual with the following criteria for choice of people to be interviewed.

The pool from which respondents were to be drawn was to consist of all accountants and engineers who worked for the company. "Accountant" and "engineer" were to be defined in terms of the work they did rather than by job titles.

It turned out to be far from easy to delimit the accounting group. Institutional accounting, unlike public accounting, has not traveled very far on the road to professional status. Many individuals in industry are called accountants; they may or may not have genuine professional duties. Our solution was to include in the sample all personnel involved in the fiscal activities of the company from the level of chief accountant or comptroller (if he were not a company officer) down to the lowest rank at which judgmental functions are exercised. Clerical workers or individuals who were primarily supervisors of clerical workers were, therefore, not included. Company officers who were also employees were excluded because we felt that their job attitudes would be complicated by their dual relationship to the organization.

The criteria for choice of engineers were much simpler than those for accountants. We included all individuals who had any design function whatsoever. Routine detail draftsmen were not included. The sample covered representatives of all the major categories of engineers: mechanical, electrical, and civil. Many of our engineers did design or technical work only. Some also had supervisory functions. All, however, functioned in some way as engineers. We did not include any with engineering background whose primary job was the supervision of production.

After a list of all individuals in the company who fitted these criteria had been assembled, the following data were requested: age, job title, some indication of level in the company, and length of service. We then went through the list and chose our respondents on a random basis. The maximum number of individuals to be interviewed in any one company was originally set at fifty; at one of the companies that limit was exceeded somewhat. When we were dealing with a very large company, our sample was chosen on a random basis. We checked the result by noting the degree to which the pattern of age, length of service, and level within our sample matched that within the population of accountants and engineers within the company as a whole. In all cases it did. In companies in which the number of potential respondents was less than fifty we interviewed everyone on the list.

Almost invariably the individuals chosen by this procedure actually were interviewed. Occasionally there would be a substitution because of the requirements of a person's job or because of vacation schedules. A very few people refused to be interviewed. Substitutions were made in such a way as to maintain the demographic characteristics of the sample. Although it was made clear that being interviewed was not to be forced on anyone, each company indicated to its staff that cooperation was favorably viewed.

Interviewing Procedure

Every effort was made to obtain good rapport with the people we interviewed. A preliminary letter went out to all of our respondents sometime before we appeared. Thus they were acquainted with the general outline of our project prior to the interview. We made every effort to dissociate ourselves from the company to assure our respondents of the confidentiality of their reports to us and to maintain our status as scientific investigators. The only indication of our success in this is to be found in the nature of the material we were able to gather. Of course, we never know what we are not told, but we certainly were told enough of a confidential nature so that it is our firm conviction that rapport with most of the people we interviewed was excellent.

After a brief introduction in which the nature of the project was explained, the interviewer informed the respondent that he was primarily interested in hearing about actual experiences. Long-range and short-range sequences of events were then defined. The respondent was told that he could "start with any kind of story you like—either a time when you felt exceptionally good or a time when you felt exceptionally bad about your job, either a long-range sequence of events or a short-range incident." After the first sequence was completely explored, the respondent was asked for a second. This time he was given somewhat less freedom to choose the kind of story. If he had given a high, he was then asked for a low; if he had given a long-range sequence, he was asked for a short-range one. Some respondents went on to tell a third story and in some cases even a fourth. The average number of sequences per respondent was 2.4. As has been indicated, the course of the interview, as each sequence was described, consisted of a search for the factors, both first-level and second-level, and the effects.

In determining the criticalness of the sequence, we followed the procedure of using a rating scale worked out in our second pilot study. After each sequence of events had been related, the interviewees were given a rating scale containing twenty-one positions. They were asked to indicate on this scale how seriously their feelings (good or bad) about their jobs had been affected by what happened. Position number one was to be used for a sequence that hardly affected their feelings at all. Position twenty-one was to be used for a sequence that affected their feelings as seriously as the most important events in their working experience. Intermediate feelings could be recorded within these extreme points. Appendix I gives the complete form of the predetermined parts of the interview. At the close of the work in each plant, a letter was sent to each respondent thanking him for his cooperation on the project.

Chapter 4   # How the Interviews Were Analyzed

From the very inception of this project we planned to apply the technique of content analysis to the stories gathered in our interviews. There are two basic approaches to content analysis. The first of these is an a priori approach in which analysis is based upon a previously defined and outlined schematic system. For example, one could approach a body of material in an attempt to sort out factual from evaluative statements. The two categories of statements would be defined beforehand, and all the material obtained would be sorted out into these two categories. Many of the analytic schemes used in the treatment of psychological tests are of this nature. Similarly, much of the content analysis used by students of public opinion falls under this heading.

The second is an a posteriori approach. In this, the categories of analysis are extracted from the material itself. As defined by Lasswell (33), this approach tends to set up categories that are meaningful in terms of the empirical material gathered during the course of the study.

It would have been possible to use either approach in our own study, but we chose the second. The list of factors and effects in job attitudes based upon our review of the literature could have provided an analytical framework. In fact, in some ways this would have eased our task considerably because of the possibility of precoding the interview material, that is, classifying it during the interview. We chose not to do so out of a feeling that the most valuable analysis would be one which emerged from the material itself. In the end our analytic scheme is not

37

really very different from that which would have been derived from an analysis of the literature; however, we feel that it is much more strongly based on the data itself and that the defining characteristics for our analytic categories are both more meaningful and more communicable.

Method for Developing the Analytic Scheme

As a first step in preparing the analytic scheme, all of the interviews were read by one of our staff members and the replies were broken down into "thought units." A thought unit is defined as a statement about a single event or condition that led to a feeling, a single characterization of a feeling, or a description of a single effect. Some examples were randomly chosen:

1. The way it was given to me showed the supervisor had confidence in my work.
2. Feel fresh and eager, ready to come to work.
3. Gave me an attitude of indifference toward my job, didn't care whether it got done or not.
4. Wasted time doing unnecessary tasks. After the job, I knew it wouldn't work, just sat there until he came back for it.
5. I like to know—there's a reason for doing the job.
6. You can see some accomplishments.

A sample of 5000 thought units of the entire total was typed in triplicate on 3 x 5 index cards. These were then sorted into piles independently by two of the staff members. The directions were, "put into the same pile the cards that seem to go together."

The two staff members who had sorted out piles of thought units now joined in examining and naming or labeling them. It was found that there were some major differences between the two sets of sorts; however, by splitting some categories and combining others, a new series of categories emerged, which was then accepted tentatively as a basis for analysis. There were, of course, three groups of categories: those for first-level factors, for second-level factors, and for effects. Each category included within itself many subcategories. These subcategories essentially involved specification of the kinds of thought units included in the major category.

Once the categorical scheme was prepared, the task of detailed analysis could begin.   Each sequence was read carefully. The factors and effects found in that sequence were identified and coded by means of the categorical scheme.   Criteria for the identification of the sequence as long-range or short-range were also developed.

In carrying out the analysis, there were occasional modifications of the scheme.   These consisted almost exclusively of the addition of new kinds of specification to each of the major categories as we found sequences of events that included thought units not present in the sample from which the scheme had been constructed.   No major modifications of the scheme took place during the course of the analysis.

In all, 476 sequences fitted our criteria for acceptability and were coded.   The first eighty-two were independently coded by two members of our staff and checked by a third.   All disagreements in coding were discussed among the three staff members, and a final concensus was reached.   Thereafter the sequences were coded by only one of our staff members and a spot check of one out of seven sequences was independently coded by another.   All sequences, whether spot checked or not, were checked by both of the other staff members in the coding group and disagreements discussed.   In the first series of thirty-seven sequences there was an average of 2.54 disagreements per sequence in thirty-nine categories on which disagreements were possible. In the next twenty-eight sequences this dropped to 1.93 disagreements; in the next sixteen sequences there were 2.0 disagreements per sequence.   With 95 per cent agreement between two independent coders and an additional check by a third person, we felt the analysis to be sufficiently objective to provide reliable data.

Chapter 5   The Definition of a Sequence of Events

O ur analysis fell into five parts. These are, first, the description of the person speaking; second, an over-all description of the sequence of events; third, the description of the objective situation in the sequence of events (first-level factors); fourth, a description of the needs, motives, and perceptions of the person speaking (second-level factors); and fifth, a description of the behavioral and other effects of his attitudes. In this chapter we describe more definitely what we mean by a sequence of events.

Before giving this description, one must know clearly what comprises an acceptable sequence of events. The following criteria were developed.

First, the sequence must revolve around an event or a series of events; that is, there must be *some* objective happening. The report cannot be concerned entirely with the speaker's psychological reactions or with his feelings.

Second, the sequence of events must be bounded in time; it should have a beginning that can be identified, a middle, and, unless the events are still going on, there must be some sort of identifiable ending, not necessarily dramatic or abrupt.

Third, the story must have taken place during a period in which feelings about the job were either exceptionally good or exceptionally bad. It may be noted, incidentally, that we were told a number of stories by individuals at very high levels that did not meet this criterion because of the marked ambivalence of feeling. In these stories extreme tension with a very deleterious effect on morale was concurrent with a high degree of positive emotional involvement in the job. A study of individuals under circumstances of such conflict would certainly be of great interest, but since it did not follow the main line of our research it was not pursued.

Fourth, the story must concern a period of time in the speaker's life when he held a position that fell within the limits of our sample. Thus a story told about a time when an engineer had been a laborer was not acceptable. However, there were exceptions to this. Stories that involve aspirations to professional work or transitions from subprofessional to professional levels were included.

Fifth, the story must be about a situation in which the speaker's feelings about his job were directly affected and not about a sequence of events that revolved around high or low spirits caused by something unrelated to the job. It is true that we accepted some stories in which personal factors played a role in the person's job attitudes. For example, we included the report of an individual who was forced by his company to move into an unfriendly community and who had a low period because of this. However, we did not include a sequence in which the sole origin of a person's attitudes was his social life, marriage, or the death of a parent.

Short- and Long-Range Sequences

Classification of each sequence as long-range or as short-range followed the basic criteria described earlier in this book (cf. Chapter 2). In our coding we found that it was easy to become confused because very often the respondent would speak in one breath of the actual duration of the events and in another of the duration of the feelings that were set into motion by the events. Classification of range was based entirely on the duration of the events; the duration of feeling was analyzed separately.

This analysis was extremely important because of a need to differentiate between short-range sequences of events which have lasting consequences and those which have not. The analysis of duration of feelings was of importance primarily for the short-range sequences, since virtually all long-range sequences involve stories in which the feelings are coincidental with the events that are being described.

Our classification included four kinds of short-range sequences.

In one, the events and feelings are approximately coincidental. There is a sharp spurt of feeling up or down that lasts approximately as long as the event itself or perhaps dies off and is terminated shortly afterwards. There is no lasting effect. The events are recalled during the interview with a kind of "cold emotion."

In a second kind of short-range sequence the feelings may persist long after the initial event. For example, a person may report that a project he suggested was turned down and that he still feels "burned up" about it.

In the third kind of short-range sequence the individual reports that although the feelings died down they are periodically re-awakened by some appropriate stimulus. For example, a man reported, "I felt terrible when I was passed over for the promotion. I got over it soon and went back to work, but every time I have to go up to the office of the man who got my job I feel terrible about it again."

A fourth kind of short-range sequence involves a change of feelings, which is initially very sharp, which then tails off, but never reverts completely to normal. For example, "When I finally knew I had the problem licked, I was absolutely higher than a kite. Of course, you go back to normal a little bit, but the good feeling persisted with me for months and made everything I did a real pleasure." These four kinds of short-range sequences were identified during the coding and each sequence was classified accordingly.

An analysis which showed some promise during our early discussions but which was not, in the end, too fruitful was the description of the way in which the sequence of events ended. We thought that the way in which the feelings ended would be of great interest to industry, since it would give some clues about handling emotional reactions to job situations. To a psychologist, the analysis of the endings of our sequences would be important, especially the lows, because they would tell us something about the way in which individuals can escape or remove themselves from frustrating situations.

The following kinds of endings were anticipated: that the feelings had dissipated spontaneously, that they had been ended by the intrusion of external factors beyond the control of the individual, or that they had ended because of successful attempts by the individual to solve the problem or to escape from the situation either physically or psychologically. In some cases, of course, we were being told about contemporaneous situations.

The Six Basic Groups

In the end, all of the information describing the sequence was used to classify each sequence of events into one of six basic groups. This classification involved three dimensions. The first of these was the direction of the affect, high or low. The second was the range of the sequence. The third was the relationship between the range of the sequence and the duration of feelings. Since all of the long-range sequences were considered to have feelings of long duration, we had six rather than the eight possible permutations of these three dimensions. These are the six groups:

1. High long-range
2. Low long-range
3. High short-range, of short duration of feelings
4. High short-range, of long duration of feelings
5. Low short-range, of short duration of feelings
6. Low short-range, of long duration of feelings

Finally, we should note that the division into long-range and short-range sequences that was so important as we were gathering the stories turned out to be of secondary significance compared to the distinction based on the duration of feelings. Therefore, most of the results are presented for the four groups of attitude duration:

1. Long duration of feelings from high long-range sequences, high short-range sequences
2. Long duration of feelings from low long-range sequences, low short-range sequences
3. Short duration of feelings from high short-range sequences
4. Short duration of feelings from low short-range sequences

Chapter 6   # The Definition of Job-Attitude Factors

In our content analysis we were attempting to isolate the ingredients in the attitude stories we were told in order that we might be able to compare different stories on the same variables. Perhaps the most important variable to consider was why the attitudes changed. We needed to know what happened and why what happened changed the attitudes of our respondents. Our factors are the terms that we decided upon to stand for things that happened and the feelings that were expressed about what happened. Since the meaning attached to these terms can and do vary considerably among different persons, it is essential that we attempt to define more specifically what we mean by each term. The definitions given below are those which our coders used.

First-Level Factors

As has been indicated before, we define a first-level factor as an objective element of the situation in which the respondent finds a source for his good or bad feelings about the job. In this section we attempt to describe the criteria for each of our categories so that the reader can understand clearly just what we mean when we refer to them in the further course of the discussion of our findings. These factors are not listed in the order of their importance but in the order of their appearance in our coding scheme.

1. Recognition. The major criterion for this category was some act of recognition to the person speaking to us. The source could be almost anyone: supervisor, some other individual in management, management as an impersonal force, a client, a peer, a professional colleague, or the general public. Some act of notice, praise, or blame was involved. We felt that this category should include what we call "negative recognition," that is, acts of criticism or blame. In our subcategories we differentiated between situations in which rewards were given along with the acts of recognition and those in which there were no concrete rewards. Note that we had many sequences in which the central event was some act, such as a promotion or a wage increase, which was not itself accompanied by verbal recognition but which was perceived by the respondent as a source of feelings of recognition. These sequences were coded under "recognition second level."

One might ask, since we had a separate category for interpersonal relations, where we coded recognition and where we coded interpersonal relations? The defining characteristic was the emphasis on the act of recognition or on the characteristics of interaction. When the story included statements characterizing the nature of the interaction between the respondent and the supervisor, peer, or subordinate, we coded the sequence as a story involving interpersonal relations. When the emphasis was merely on the act of recognition, this was not done.

2. *Achievement.* Our definition of achievement also included its opposite, failure, and the absence of achievement. Stories involving some specifically mentioned success were put into this category and these included the following: successful completion of a job, solutions to problems, vindication, and seeing the results of one's work.

3. *Possibility of growth.* The inclusion of a possibility as an objective factor in the situation may sound paradoxical, but there were some sequences in which the respondent told us of changes in his situation involving objective evidences that the possibilities for his growth were now increased or decreased. An example of this is a change in status that officially included a likelihood that the respondent would be able to rise in a company, or the converse. For example, if a man moves from a craftsman's position to that of a draftsman, the new status opens up a previously closed door; he may eventually rise to the position of design engineer or perhaps even project engineer. When the respondent told us that this had been clearly presented to him as part of his change, then possibility of growth was certainly considered as a

first-level factor. Similarly, when an individual was told that his lack of formal education made it impossible for him ever to advance in the company, "negative" possibility for growth was coded.

Possibility for growth, however, has another connotation. It includes not only the likelihood that the individual would be able to move onward and upward within his organization but also a situation in which he is able to advance in his own skills and in his profession. Thus, included in this category were stories in which a new element in the situation made it possible for the respondent to learn new skills or to acquire a new professional outlook.

4. Advancement. This category was used only when there was an actual change in the status or position of the person in the company. In situations in which an individual transferred from one part of the company to another without any change in status but with increased opportunities for responsible work, the change was considered an increased responsibility (for which we have a category) but not formally an advancement.

5. Salary. This category included all sequences of events in which compensation plays a role. Surprisingly enough, virtually all of these involve wage or salary increases, or unfulfilled expectation of salary increases.

6. Interpersonal relations. One might expect that interpersonal relations would pervade almost all of the sequences. They do play a role, necessarily, in situations involving recognition or changes in status within the company or company and management policies; however, we restricted our coding of interpersonal relations to those stories in which there was some actual verbalization about the characteristics of the interaction between the person speaking and some other individual. We set this up in terms of three major categories:

Interpersonal relations—superior
Interpersonal relations—subordinate
Interpersonal relations—peers

Within each of these categories we used a series of subcategories, which can be found in Appendix 2, to describe various kinds of situations involving interaction between the person speaking and others. These subcategories would have enabled us to differentiate between the characteristics of interpersonal relationships which are purely social and those which were "sociotechnical," as defined by J. A. C. Brown (9). A sociotechnical story involves interpersonal relationships that arise when people interact in the performance of their jobs. A "purely social" story would relate interactions that might take place within working hours and on the premises of work but independent of the activities of the job. A coffee-break friendship or a water-cooler feud would be examples. As it turned out, we had virtually no stories of the purely social kind. Whether this was due in some way to the set produced by our interviewing instructions, whether this is a characteristic of the level of people we spoke to, or whether in actuality the nature of extra-job interpersonal relationships in the plant does not play so great a role as has been assumed is not at present possible to determine.

7. *Supervision-technical.* Although it is difficult to divorce the characteristics of interpersonal relationships with one's supervisor from his behavior in carrying out his job, it seemed to us that it was not an impossible task. We were able, with a high degree of reliability among independent coders, to identify those sequences of events that revolved around the characteristics of interpersonal relationships and those, classified under the category supervision-technical, in which the competence or incompetence, fairness or unfairness of the supervisor were the critical characteristics. Statements about the supervisor's willingness or unwillingness to delegate responsibility or his willingness or unwillingness to teach would be classified under this category. A supervisor who is perpetually nagging or critical and a supervisor who kept things humming smoothly and efficiently might both be reported as factors in a sequence of events that led to exceptional feelings about the job.

8. *Responsibility.* Factors relating to responsibility and authority are covered in this category, which includes those sequences of events in which the person speaking reported that he derived satisfaction from being given responsibility for his own work or for the work of others or being given new responsibility. It also includes stories in which there was a loss of satisfaction or a negative attitude towards the job stemming from a lack of responsibility. In cases, however, in which the story revolved around a wide gap between a person's authority and the authority he needed to carry out his job responsibilities the factor identified was "company policy and administration." The rationale for

this was that such a discrepancy between authority and job responsibilities would be considered evidence of poor management.

9. Company policy and administration. This category describes those components of a sequence of events in which some over-all aspect of the company was a factor. We identified two kinds of over-all company policy and administration characteristics. One involved the adequacy or inadequacy of company organization and management. Thus there can exist a situation in which a man has lines of communication crossing in such a way that he does not really know for whom he is working, in which he has inadequate authority for satisfactory completion of his task, or in which a company policy is not carried out because of inadequate organization of the work.

The second kind of over-all characteristic of the company involved not inadequacy but the harmfulness or beneficial effects of the company's policies. These are primarily personnel policies. These policies, when viewed negatively, are not described as ineffective, but rather as "malevolent."

10. Working conditions. This category was used for stories in which the physical conditions of work, the amount of work, or the facilities available for doing the work were mentioned in the sequence of events. Adequacy or inadequacy of ventilation, lighting, tools, space, and other such environmental characteristics would be included here.

11. Work itself. Work itself was used when the respondent mentioned the actual doing of the job or the tasks of the job as a source of good or bad feelings about it. Thus jobs can be routine or varied, creative or stultifying, overly easy or overly difficult. The duties of a position can include an opportunity to carry through an entire operation or they can be restricted to one minute aspect of it.

12. Factors in personal life. As previously indicated, we did not accept sequences in which a factor in the personal life of an individual having nothing to do with his job was responsible for a period of good or bad feelings, even if these feelings affected the job. We did accept situations in which some aspect of the job affected personal life in such a way that the effect was a factor in the respondent's feelings about his job. For example, if the company demanded that a man move to a new location in a community in which the man's family was unhappy, this was accepted as a valid sequence of events and was coded under the "personal life" category. Similarly, family needs for salary and other family problems stemming from the job situation were acceptable.

13. Status. It would have been easy to slip into the trap of inferring status consideration from other factors. For example, it might be considered that any advancement would involve a change in status and ought to be thus coded. This was not done. "Status" was coded only when the respondent actually mentioned some sign or appurtenance of status as being a factor in his feelings about the job. Thus a person who spoke of having a secretary in his new position, of being allowed to drive a company car, or of being unable to use a company eating facility gave us a story coded under this category.

14. Job security. Here again we were not dealing with feelings of security, since these were coded as second-level factors, but with objective signs of presence or absence of job security. Thus we included such considerations as tenure and company stability or instability, which reflected in some objective way on a person's job security.

Second-Level Factors

The material analyzed for second-level factors came from a respondent's answer to the question, "What did these events mean to you?" In essence he was looking at himself, trying to figure out what in his own need and value systems led to his attitude towards his job at the time of the events being described. Different respondents were more or less successful in this self-examination. Our information about second-level factors is limited by the extent to which each respondent could verbalize his feelings and the extent to which responses given were based on stereotypes of the socially acceptable or on real perceptions. In the end we were limited by our respondents' capacity for self-insight. As with all of our material, we had to work with what people told us; we did not know what they were unable to tell or refused to divulge.

In one of our most valuable analyses we identified the first-level factor or factors from which the respondent derived his feelings. Thus a feeling of recognition could come from words of praise, from a promotion or raise, or from a new job assignment.

Any of these could mean to the respondent that his merit had been recognized. The identification of these derivations was based not on inferences but on the subjects' own verbal responses. For each sequence of events the second-level factors were identified and the derivation of each from the first-level factors was indicated.

No detailed description of the analytical scheme for second-level factors is necessary, since the words are used in their dictionary meanings and the specifications given in the analytical scheme (cf. Appendix 2) are limited to such directions as "recognition second level." These are the subcategories for this one factor:

1. First-level factors perceived as a source of feelings of recognition

2. First-level factors perceived as a source of failure to obtain recognition

3. First-level factors perceived as a source of disapproval

The remainder of the subcategories are given in Appendix 2

The entire list of second-level factors follows:

1. Feelings of recognition

2. Feelings of achievement

3. Feelings of possible growth, blocks to growth, first-level factors perceived as evidence of actual growth

4. Feelings of responsibility, lack of responsibility or diminished responsibility

5. Group feelings: feelings of belonging or isolation, sociotechnical or purely social

6. Feelings of interest or lack of interest in the performance of the job

7. Feelings of increased or decreased status

8. Feelings of increased or decreased security

9. Feelings of fairness or unfairness

10. Feelings of pride or of inadequacy or guilt

11. Feelings about salary *

* This factor was included to cover those situations in which the first-level factor was viewed primarily as a source of the things that money can bring. If an answer to the question, "Why did this promotion make you feel good?" was, "I like the idea of being able to make more money," then the second-level factor was coded "salary."

Chapter 7

The Definition
of the Effects
# of Job Attitudes

The analysis of effects was relatively simple, since most effects were specified by the respondent in concrete terms. When the respondents did not freely mention the effects of their changed job attitudes, they were elicited by the following questions:

1. Did these feelings affect the way you did your job? How? How long did this go on?

2. Can you give me a specific example of the way in which your performance on the job was affected? How long?

3. Did what happened affect you personally in any way? How long?

4. Did what happened affect the way you felt about working at that company, or did it merely make you feel good or bad about the occurrence itself?

5. Did the consequences of what happened at this time affect your career? How?

6. Did what happened change the way you felt about your profession? How?

Our major-effect categories include most of the criterion measures which have been studied in the literature of industrial psychology, as well as some other criteria which have not been so clearly defined in the past.

1. Performance effects. There were three kinds of performance effects given by our respondents. In one, the respondent made a general comment identifying the period as one in which work was either better or poorer than usual; however, he gave no specific illustration of the precise nature of the change. Although these general comments were our least reliable data, they did indicate that the person perceived himself as working better or worse. We have decided, therefore, to include these general statements as performance effects.

In the second we were told about changes in the rate of work but not in its quality. Thus we were told in more or less concrete terms that the respondent had slowed down or had speeded up his output. For example, an engineer told us about the speed with which he was able to turn out a set of drawings for a new design during a high period or an accountant told of dragging out the preparation of a report during a low.

The third kind of performance effect consisted of reports of changes in the quality of work. These were often very concrete. We were told of changes in the ability to solve problems or, contrariwise, of situations in which negative feelings toward the job led to work that the respondent knew was sloppy and beneath the level of which he was capable.

An additional category had to be included to cover those cases in which the response to the question, "Did this affect the way you did your job?" was not a simple negative but an affirmative statement of the fact that the respondent never let his feelings about the job interfere with the way he did his work. This was a fairly common statement. It is hard to know whether this represents the actual effect of professional pride in preventing the lowering of standards in work or whether it represents self-justification and rationalization.

2. Turnover. There is a continuum of possible categories under this general heading. At one end, we have situations in which the respondent actually quit his job. At the other, we have situations in which positive feelings were so great that the respondent turned down attractive offers elsewhere. Within these two extremes we have many statements about turnover. Respondents in periods of negative job attitudes will make connections and have interviews; or they may not go so far but may read the want ads in the newspapers and "talk around." A somewhat weaker statement, but one which still carries some weight, is, "Thought of quitting but didn't do anything about it." In our statistical analysis of effects it was always possible to separate out the concrete behavioral effects, such as actually quitting or making connections, from effects in sequences in which the respondent merely "thought about quitting." Lastly, we were occasionally told about situations in which the events described did not lead to an immediate decision to leave but played a role in a later determination to change jobs.

3. Mental health effects. The effect of job situations on the mental health of our respondents was evident in many of our interviews. There were some positive effects. These included statements of improvement in tension symptoms, of gaining weight when underweight, and of a cessation of such harmful activities as excessive drinking and smoking.

The bulk of our reports in this category is, however, negative. We were able to distinguish three classes of negative mental-health effects. The first of these, and the most serious, although rare, were psychosomatic effects. These occurred in sequences of events in which the respondent himself drew a connection between the tensions of the job and the appearance of skin ailments, gastrointestinal ailments, such as ulcers, and cardiac conditions. We were extremely parsimonious in using this category, restricting it to situations in which the respondent reported himself clinically ill and under the care of a physician.

The second category included stories in which we were told of physiological changes related to tensions; these changes produced real physical symptoms but did not lead to a diagnosis of pathology. Examples are nausea, vomiting, severe headaches, and marked loss of appetite. Loss of sleep was categorized separately, since it was reported fairly frequently as the only symptom of a change in mental health.

Lastly, we noted the more diffuse symptoms resulting from tension. These included many manifestations of anxiety states. It was, of course, impossible during an hour's interview to probe at all deeply into the dynamics of the respondent's personality. We cannot, therefore, assess the relative contribution of job tensions and of underlying neurotic trends. However, we can report on the frequency with which people describe these anxiety states as resulting from the pressures of the job.

4. Effects on interpersonal relationships. In the form of the interview used in the major study, we asked the respondent about the effects on interpersonal relationships manifested during the period under discussion. These can be categorized as improvements or as degeneration in interpersonal relationships. Thus a man might report that as a result of tensions on the job he got along less well with his wife, that he was snappish or irritable with his children, or that he was seclusive and avoided the company of his friends. On the contrary, he might report that as a result of good feelings about his job he had become "more bearable at home" and had found new pleasure in his relationship with his children. We were also told of many instances in which there were effects on interpersonal relationships on the job.

5. Attitudinal effects. There were many reports of situations in which a person's feelings about his job led to changed attitudes towards himself, his colleagues, his profession, or the company for which he worked. We felt that both positive and negative statements of this kind were worthy of identification and analysis. The category of "attitudinal effects" was set up in order to permit us to identify these statements and to estimate the frequency of their occurrence among different situations and for different kinds of people.

PART II · The Results

The results of this study are presented under three general headings. The first, and most extensive, section consists of data relating to the factors that lead to positive and negative attitudes toward the job. It will be recalled that the major question this study set out to investigate was whether different kinds of factors were responsible for bringing about job satisfaction and job dissatisfaction. We were further interested in the nature of these different factors and in discovering general psychological principles to account for the differences, if they occurred. What were the objective first-level factors that occurred during the periods of low attitudes described to us by our engineers and accountants? Are they different from the factors that occurred during their high job attitudes? Are the factors that account for short-range attitude changes different from those that cause changes of attitudes of a long duration? Are changes in job attitudes the result of specific factors operating alone, or are some combinations more meaningful? Why did our respondents' attitudes change? In other words, what does an examination of the second-level factors appearing in the stories show? Chapter 8 presents the findings relating to these questions.

In Chapter 9 are recorded the results about the effects of these attitudes. How is job performance affected by positive job attitudes as opposed to negative job attitudes? How frequently do people quit when the satisfactions from their jobs decrease sharply? If they do not actually quit, what are their thoughts about remaining with the company? What happens to the image of the company in the minds of employees when their job satisfactions change? What kinds of mental-health effects occur? Specifically what kinds of changes in interpersonal relations take place at the time job satisfactions change? These are questions for which data from our study are applicable.

We complete the presentation of our findings in Chapter 10, in which we explore the data on individual differences. This chapter focuses on such questions as: Are the factors that make engineers happy or unhappy different from those affecting accountants? Are they affected differently? How important is age, education, job level, and experience in determining what will make an employee happy or unhappy?

These three chapters present the evidence from our study for the theory of job motivation that follows. Other sources to substantiate this theory are included in the chapter on perspectives in which we attempt to apply the theory to the world of work and to some of the problems of society in general.

Chapter 8   The Factors

W e begin the examination of the results with the data from
the high sequences. These are followed by the findings from the
low sequences of events. For both highs and lows the first-level
factors are presented and then discussed in the light of the data
from analysis of the range of sequences, second-level factors, and
a study of interrelationships among factors. After each group
has been separately presented, the high and lows are compared.

The High Sequences: First-Level Factors

Table 1 lists each of the first-level factors in the order of their
frequency of appearance in the 228 high job-attitude sequences.
The table is separated into four parts: (1) *achievement and
recognition;* (2) *work itself, responsibility,* and *advancement;*
(3) *salary;* and (4) a set of ten infrequently appearing factors.
There is a significance in this grouping for the understanding of
what makes people happy with their jobs. Further explanation
is developed in the ensuing paragraphs.

The most frequent factor appearing in these 228 sequences is
achievement. It appears in 41 per cent of the sequences of events
that accompanied favorable job attitudes. Each one of this group
of stories revolves about successful completion of a job. The
jobs themselves are varied. A marine engineer told about the
time he succeeded in designing a new kind of screw propeller for
a completely new kind of boat. Another engineer told about the
impressive achievements involved in building a new type of atomic
reactor. Accountants, too, are highly achievement-oriented. In
the mushrooming growth of industry accountancy is in process of
becoming professionalized. We heard many stories of achieve-

TABLE 1

Percentage of Each First-Level Factor Appearing in High Attitude Sequences

N = 228

Factor	Total *
1. Achievement	41
2. Recognition	33
3. Work itself	26
4. Responsibility	23
5. Advancement	20
6. Salary	15
7. Possibility of growth	6
8. Interpersonal relations—subordinate	6
9. Status	4
10. Interpersonal relations—superior	4
11. Interpersonal relations—peers	3
12. Supervision-technical	3
13. Company policy and administration	3
14. Working conditions	1
15. Personal life	1
16. Job security	1

* The percentages total more than 100 per cent, since more than one factor can appear in any single sequence of events.

ment revolving around the introduction of new cost-accounting schemes, of machine processing of data, and of successful integration of accounting into production control.

Second in the order of frequency of mention is recognition, which appeared in one third of the high job-attitude stories. As previously described, recognition can come from many sources: supervisors, peers, customers, or subordinates. An important aspect of the effectiveness of recognition for producing high job attitudes is some achievement as a basis for the recognition. The evidence for this association and its implications are discussed later. For example, an accountant told of working for a few hours with a representative from the company's district office, showing him what was done in the accountant's department. The visitor later told the accountant's boss that he was impressed with the presentation and that he thought the accountant was doing a good job. The boss passed along the compliment. This came as quite a surprise, since the accountant had worked for this company for years and this was the first time he had been recognized by anything but raises. "Biggest thing," he said, "was the personal satisfaction with the job done and then a pat on the back."

Each one of the next group of factors—work itself, responsibility, and advancement—appeared in at least one fifth of the high sequences. For the work itself category our respondents described aspects of their jobs which gave them tremendous satisfactions. These aspects were related to the nature of their work and were rewarding in themselves with or without specific achievement or recognition. Frequently cited desiderata were creative or challenging work, varied work, and an opportunity to do a job completely from beginning to end. An illustrative story was told by a design draftsman in his middle thirties. At the time of our interview he was doing "creative" design work which enabled the company to make money. He said, "I'm doing creative work and this keeps me content and happy. In another year I won't be creating and then my work is not satisfying and I don't do a good job and I'll quit." He had been through this experience in another company and had even accepted a salary cut to return to the present company where he felt he could do creative work. His good feelings lasted until he was put on a routine job again.

Responsibility is the fourth in the list of factors ranked in Table 1. The themes of the stories in which this factor was coded include being allowed to work without supervision, being responsible for one's own efforts, being given responsibility for work of others, and being given a new kind of job, with new responsibilities but with no formal advancement. We may note that the last situation in which, for example, a draftsman takes on the duties and responsibilities of a project engineer without the status is not necessarily either good or bad. Nevertheless, this kind of story often appeared as a high sequence. That is, the lack of formal promotion did not remove the good feelings and good results stemming from the increase in responsibility. Stature is evidently more important to our population than status. The following story exemplifies this. An accountant in his early forties was working in a department in which the bookkeeper had been drafted. Despite the accountant's limited experience, the job was turned over to him on a more or less temporary basis. He was not given the bookkeeper's title, and he received only a very small salary increase, but it was an opportunity to show that he could do the work. He reported, "It made me feel as though I were making progress . . . and that I was on the right track." Determined to prove that he had the necessary ability, he studied nights to learn more about the job, offered ideas for improvement, and put in long hours without reimbursement.

Fifth in the list of factors appearing in the high sequences is advancement. This factor is self-explanatory; the employee was promoted. It is interesting that in almost half of these stories the advancement was unexpected. The power of a promotion to increase job satisfaction is often related to feelings of growth, recognition, achievement, responsibility (see discussion of second-level factors). A typical example of a promotion that came unexpectedly and offered all the factors just mentioned was given by one of our engineers. His age, experience, and seniority were against him, but a job was especially created and given to him, along with an unexpected salary increase. His superiors also paid him all sorts of compliments in telling him why they had selected him for the job. He was pleased and surprised mainly because it indicated to him that his work was appreciated and that his superiors had confidence in him. The job itself was an important one, full of new details and responsibility. It involved another side of engineering that he found more interesting than what he had been doing. The promotion "strengthened his ties with the company." He subsequently had opportunities to leave but was content there and after many years still feels good because of that promotion. Again, as with responsibility, we find in this story the secondary nature of increased income as a factor involved in increasing the engineer's job satisfaction.

As we can see from the list of sixteen factors in Table 1, only the five factors described above seem to play an important role in increasing the job satisfaction of the accountants and engineers in our sample. Salary was the only other factor that appeared with any significant frequency in the stories that described highpoints in job satisfaction. It is listed separately because it belongs in a different group of factors as far as its psychological effects on job attitudes is concerned. We must present further information before we can adequately understand the meaning of salary as a factor producing favorable job attitudes.

If we contrast the top five factors with the other eleven in the list, including salary, we can note that the top five focus on the job itself: (1) on doing the job, (2) on liking the job, (3) on success in doing the job, (4) on recognition for doing the job, and (5) on moving upward as an indication of professional growth.

The factors that are rarely instrumental in bringing about high job attitudes focus not on the job itself but rather on the characteristics of the context in which the job is done: working conditions, interpersonal relationships, supervision, company policies, administration of these policies, effects on the worker's personal life, job security, and salary. This is a basic distinction. The satisfiers relate to the *actual job*. Those factors that do not act as satisfiers describe the *job situation*. Another point should be noted for later comparisons with the results from the low job-attitude stories. Only one third of the factors we identified are involved in bringing about job satisfaction (holding in abeyance for the while the factor of salary). Thus there are only a few interrelated factors that are effective as satisfiers.

1. Long-range versus short-range attitude changes. We now have a picture of the kinds of situations that lead to highly positive attitudes toward the job. Can we add anything to this picture by an analysis of the information that was given to us through the use of other questions than those directly related to the objective situation? First, are there any valuable data to be found from a search of the material relating to the range of sequences?

It will be recalled that we divided the sequences of events into six basic groups, three of which were appropriate to the highs. Of these three, one consists of stories that described very specific and short-term events and for which the feelings that were aroused by these events terminated very quickly (short-range sequence—short-term attitudes). The other two groups consist of stories in which either a specific event or a long series of events had lasting effects on feelings (short-range—long term attitudes and long-range sequences). Clearly, the latter two kinds of events were of greater significance to the over-all psychological economy of the individual.

Table 2 shows an interesting fact about this division. Among the short-range sequences the frequency of short-range attitudes is much smaller for the highs than for the lows. Good feelings about the job tend to persist long after the specific events which aroused them have passed. Although bad feelings related to

TABLE 2

Distribution of Sequences among the Six Duration Categories

High		Low	
	N		N
Short-range short-term attitudes	39	Short-range short-term attitudes	72
Short-range long-term attitudes	100	Short-range long-term attitudes	53
Long-range attitudes	89	Long-range attitudes	123
Total	228	Total	248

long-range sequences of events are frequently reported, when poor job attitudes arise from a short-range event, the feelings tend to dissipate significantly more frequently than they tend to linger on. This is in contrast to good feelings about the jobs, which tend to persist, no matter how momentary the events that led to the attitude.

In Table 3 we have added a breakdown of the results of the sixteen factors for sequences which lead to long-term favorable attitudes and for sequences which result in attitude changes of a short duration. We are dealing here with the duration of feelings and not with the length of time that the sequences of events encompassed. The long-range attitudes in this table include both short- and long-range sequences.

The factors of work itself, responsibility, and advancement are almost always associated with long-term changes in job attitudes. Rarely do they cause a change that is merely transient. Contrariwise, changes in job attitudes resulting from events involving achievement or recognition are significantly more often of a short-range variety. Work itself, responsibility, and advancement are more singularly potent, as measured by their lasting effects, than either recognition or achievement. Since long-range attitude changes are also associated with greater performance effects, as shown in the next chapter, the former trio of factors are also more singularly potent for improving job effectiveness. This does not mean that achievement and recognition are not important to positive job attitudes. They are still the most frequent-appearing factors for all kinds of sequences.

When we compare the two short-term satisfiers, recognition and achievement, achievement is the more important of the two. Evidence for this distinction comes from two sets of facts from our data. First, the ratio between long-range and short-range attitude duration favors the factor of achievement. Percentages shown in Table 3 are for recognition, 64 per cent short-term changes to positive attitudes as opposed to 27 per cent long-range positive-attitude changes. The corresponding values for the achievement factor is 54 per cent associated with short-range positive-attitude change and 38 per cent with long-range attitude change. This difference in ratios is statistically significant.

TABLE 3

Percentage of Each First-Level Factor Appearing in Long-Range and Short-Range High Attitude Sequences

	Duration of Feelings	
Factor	(N = 184) Long *	(N = 39) Short
1. Achievement	38	54
2. Recognition	27	64
3. Work itself	31	3
4. Responsibility	28	0
5. Advancement	23	3
6. Salary	15	13
7. Possibility of growth	7	0
8. Interpersonal relations—subordinate	6	3
9. Status	5	3
10. Interpersonal relations—superior	4	5
11. Interpersonal relations—peers	4	0
12. Supervision-technical	3	0
13. Company policy and administration	3	0
14. Working conditions	1	0
15. Personal life	1	0
16. Job security	1	0

* The column under Long includes the frequency of lasting attitudes resulting from both long-range and short-range sequences.

TABLE 4

Interrelationships among Most Frequent First-Level Factors in the Highs *

			Percentage of Appearance
Recognition	with	achievement	61
Achievement	with	recognition	49
		responsibility	21
		work itself	32
Advancement	with	salary	24
		work itself	50
Salary	with	advancement	32
		work itself	20
Responsibility	with	recognition	21
		achievement	37
		work itself	49
Work itself	with	recognition	20
		achievement	51
		advancement	20
		responsibility	44

* This table gives the percentage frequency with which the factors on the left occurred in sequences in which the factors on the right were also found.

2. Interrelationship of factors. The second source of evidence for the distinction between recognition and achievement comes from an examination of the factors that appeared together in the stories. In Table 4 we show the interrelationship of the six major factors. In those sequences in which recognition was coded 61 per cent of the time achievement also appeared, whereas less than half the time that achievement was coded recognition was also coded. In other words, achievement is more independent of recognition than recognition is independent of achievement. In addition, achievement is shown to be more frequently associated than is recognition in the stories with the two long-range factors of responsibility and work itself.

3. Second-level factors. So far we have been discussing the findings as they come from our attempts to analyze the situations that obtained during the time when our respondents experienced a change in job attitudes. The first-level factors represent our coding of the objective events. We have been attempting to search for some systematization of what affects people's job attitudes by examining what had happened when job attitudes changed. Thus far the only feelings the respondents have revealed to us have been their high or low over-all job attitudes. Other than this, they were reporters of events. Now we turn to the results we found when we concerned ourselves not with the objective events but with the interpretation that our respondents gave of these events.

Table 5 presents the frequencies with which each of the second-level factors appears in our stories. As in the first-level factors, recognition and achievement top the list for the high sequences of events. A feeling that you have achieved and a feeling that you have been recognized are the two most frequent feelings that are associated with an increase in job satisfaction.

TABLE 5

Percentage of Each Second-Level Factor Appearing in High Job-Attitude Sequences

	Duration of Feelings		
	Long *	Short	Total
1. Recognition	57	64	59
2. Achievement	57	56	57
3. Possible growth	42	18	38
4. Advancement	3	3	3
5. Responsibility	33	18	30
6. Group feeling	11	8	10
7. Work itself	33	8	29
8. Status	21	5	18
9. Security	7	5	7
10. Fairness-unfairness	2	5	3
11. Pride, guilt, inadequacy	9	10	9
12. Salary	22	5	19

* The Long column includes the frequency of lasting attitudes resulting from both long-range and short-range sequences.

A major concept is to be found in the second-level factor, possibility of growth. Here the events that occurred had significance to the individual in terms of giving him feelings that he was progressing in his occupational life. In contrast to recognition and achievement, where long-range and short-range attitude changes are of about equal frequency, the factor of possible growth shows more than a two-to-one ratio in favor of the long-range positive changes in feelings toward a job. The great frequency with which this need was verbalized indicates that the feeling that personal or professional growth was possible bulked very large in the psychological reactions of the individual to the kinds of situations he described as central to a high.

The category possibility of growth appeared as a first-level factor quite rarely. In this category were placed stories in which objective evidence was given of the possibility of future advancement or of future changes of a positive sort in the kind of work the respondent would be doing. Thus one would expect that individuals involved in company training programs, in which theoretically the individuals are being groomed for higher positions, would report on these. The fact that our sample, which was drawn from companies that have active training programs and active rotation programs, so rarely mentioned these reasons for feeling good is indicative of the relatively slight degree to which these programs have had an effect, at least at the job level at which we were working. It seems incongruous that programs that on the face of it would appear to relate directly to one of the basic needs of employees, as drawn from this study, should so infrequently appear in our stories. As explored in the final chapter, the incongruity comes from a lack of understanding of the basic psychology of the meaning of work.

Long-range attitude changes are also seen for the next two factors in order of frequency: responsibility and work itself. Status and salary appear in somewhat less than one fifth of the high sequence stories. Here we have the individual feeling good because he was making more money and his position in the company had visibly improved.

4. *The character of the highs.* We should like to argue that the basic complex among the highs is a series of events related to feelings of self-actualization and growth. Our data show that good feelings from specific acts of verbal recognition (the "pat on the back") are more often than not only of short duration.

However, more basic feelings of recognition are associated with the positive reinforcements of advancement, added responsibility, and interesting and challenging work. Acts of verbal recognition and specific achievements can act as a kind of partial reinforcer of the basic goals which have been described by our respondents. We can consider a short range–short sequence as representing a sort of subreward, which indicates to the individual worker that he is progressing toward his basic goal. To the extent that these subrewards temporarily reinforce this long-range progression, they are a source for positive attitudes toward the job. However, the long-range goals of the individual are defined by the complex of achievement-responsibility-work itself-advancement. As Table 4 shows, these factors are highly interrelated. When some or all of the factors are present in the job situation of an individual, the fulfillment of his basic needs is such that he enters a period of exceptionally positive feelings about his job.

Analysis of the criticalness ratings supports this point of view to a limited extent. Of the factors important in the highs, recognition, achievement, and responsibility do not show any greater tendency to occur in sequences rated as highly critical than in those labeled moderately critical. However, both advancement and work itself do occur very much more frequently in the highly critical sequences. For advancement plus work itself these differences are statistically significant (.01 level). The notion that most of the sequences coded recognition and a considerable number of the sequences coded achievement represent partial reinforcers of the person's basic needs is consonant with the even distribution of these sequences along the criticalness scale. The fact that sequences involving added responsibility are not more frequently found on the high end of the criticalness scale is the sole datum that does not support our point of view.

One further note about the interrelationships of factors. Achievement can stand independently of recognition as a source of good feelings about the job. Recognition is somewhat more rarely independent of achievement. It occurs infrequently without an accompanying achievement; achievement occurs far more frequently without accompanying acts of recognition. However, one can note that achievement almost always leads to feelings of fulfillment of one kind or another. This should support our notion that the act of recognition not related to a specific sense of achievement or personal growth is a relatively trivial reason for good feelings about the job.

5. *Summary of the highs.* In summary, we have several clear-cut findings about the character of the high sequences. First, only a small number of factors, and these highly interrelated, are responsible for good feelings about the job. Second, all of the factors responsible for good feelings about the job relate to the doing of the job itself or to the intrinsic content of the job rather than to the context in which the job is done. Third, the good feelings about the job stemming from these factors are predominantly lasting rather than temporary in nature. Fourth, when good feelings about the job are temporary in nature, they stem from specific achievements and recognition of these specific achievements. Fifth, an analysis of second-level factors leads us to the conclusions that a sense of personal growth and of self-actualization is the key to an understanding of positive feelings about the job. We would define the first-level factors of achievement-responsibility-work itself-advancement as a complex of factors leading to this sense of personal growth and self-actualization. In a later discussion of these data we postulate a basic need for these goals as a central phenomenon in understanding job attitudes. That part of our data which describes short-term positive feelings about the job can be specified as due to partial reinforcements of these basic needs. These partial reinforcements stem from specific achievements and from acts of recognition. Sixth, we have acquired some data about the role of money in people's attitudes towards their jobs. However, the discussion of this important phenomenon is delayed to a later section.

The Low Sequences: First-Level Factors

We turn now to the analysis of the low sequences. From our original hypothesis concerning the distinction between "satisfiers" and "dissatisfiers" we would predict that the five factors described in the preceding section as basic to job satisfaction would be found very infrequently in the stories describing events associated with job dissatisfaction. Instead, we would expect the major contributors to job dissatisfaction to be among the other eleven factors studied; these have been characterized as describing the context in which the job is done. That this prediction proves to be true is shown by the analysis of the data on factors in low sequences given in Table 6.

We first describe the relative frequency of the different factors appearing in the low job-attitude stories. In a following section the data from second-level factors and interrelationships are presented.

Company policy and administration is the single most important factor determining bad feelings about a job. Approximately one third of the low sequences included this factor. There are two aspects to company policy and administration. In one the stories revolve around company ineffectiveness, produced by inefficiency, waste, duplication of effort, or a struggle for power. To illustrate, we can cite the report of an accounting supervisor who was continually being by-passed. Instructions pertaining to his department went out to everyone except him. A procedure was set up for a job that he was to supervise, but by the time the papers came to him his subordinates were already doing this work. The boss was busy and the accountant couldn't get to him to discuss the matter. He reports, "I couldn't figure out why I was by-passed. I felt left out and embarrassed. It was negligence on their part for not informing me about what I needed to know to do my job." As a consequence, he slowed down in his work, putting jobs off if they weren't essential.

In the second kind of story, which accounted for somewhat more than one half of these sequences, the key is not so much the ineffectiveness of the company as the deleterious effects of its policies. These include personnel and other policies that are viewed as unfair or that in some way have detrimental effects on the respondent or his co-workers. The most typical story revolved around the worker who claimed that his own career had been blighted because of company policy that gave preferment to college-educated rather than to noncollege-educated engineers and accountants. This kind of situation is inevitable, of course, in a period in which there is a major shift in growing professionalization in a field. An older generation that had its start at the clerk's or draftsman's desk is replaced by the fresh young graduates of professional schools. There was not so much bitterness against the young men with degrees, but there was a feeling that it was unfair of the company to disregard individual merit and to place sole emphasis on formal educational requirements. Unfair salary policies also came in for a great deal of criticism.

TABLE 6

Percentage of Each First-Level Factor Appearing in High and Low Job-Attitude Sequences

Duration of Feelings

	High			Low		
	Long *	Short	Total	Long *	Short	Total
1. Achievement	38	54	41 †	6	10	7
2. Recognition	27	64	33 †	11	38	18
3. Work itself	31	3	26 †	18	4	14
4. Responsibility	28	0	23 †	6	4	6
5. Advancement	23	3	20 †	14	6	11
6. Salary	15	13	15	21	8	17
7. Possibility of growth	7	0	6	11	3	8
8. Interpersonal relations—subordinate	6	3	6	1	8	3
9. Status	5	3	4	6	1	4
10. Interpersonal relations—superior	4	5	4	18	10	15 †
11. Interpersonal relations—peers	4	0	3	7	10	8 †
12. Supervision-technical	3	0	3	23	13	20 †
13. Company policy and administration	3	0	3	37	18	31 †
14. Working conditions	1	0	1	12	8	11 †
15. Personal life	1	0	1	8	7	6 †
16. Job security	1	0	1	2	0	1

* The Long column includes the frequency of lasting attitudes resulting from both long-range and short-range sequences.

† Differences of totals between high and low statistically significant at .01 level of confidence.

In more than one quarter of the low sequences involving company policy and administration salary was also mentioned as a factor.

The same kind of company ineffectiveness that leads to bad feelings can be found in the performance of individual supervisors. Technical supervision is second in the order of frequency of factors leading to low job attitudes. These stories revolve not around social relationships but around the working relationships of people with their supervisors. We were told of bungling and inefficient supervisors who were unable to schedule work or who, through lack of teaching ability, failed to inspire their people. The single most frequent failing of the supervisor cited as a reason for lows was his lack of competence in carrying out his function.

As might be expected, in many of the stories describing the poor technical qualities of supervision the interpersonal relations with the supervisors were also poor. This factor, however, appeared in fewer of the stories than technical supervision, 15 per cent as compared to 20 per cent of the 248 low-attitude sequences. This does seem surprising in view of the current concern with the way supervisors handle people. However, when deteriorated interpersonal relationships between supervisor and subordinate do occur, the effects can be devastating to the employee. An extreme example was the report from one of the accountants. His supervisor constantly criticized him in front of others, made sarcastic personal remarks, and tried to claim control over him twenty-four hours a day. He recalled that when his wife gave birth to twins he began passing out cigars only to have his supervisor order him back to the job. As a result, the situation "got on his nerves" so much that he developed chronic nausea and his doctor recommended that he quit.

Recognition was coded in almost one fifth of the low stories we were told. They include a wide variety of reports in which a component of the situation is the failure of the respondent to receive recognition for work he has done. Examples are the man who felt aggrieved because whenever he wrote a report his superior signed it or the man who worked hard on a new accounting system only to have it summarily turned down because the company then decided it did not need a new system. One interesting point should be raised here. Although stories in which recognition was obtained occurred far more frequently than stories in which there was a failure to obtain recognition, a great many of our respondents prefaced their stories with the comment that "no one gives you a pat on the back around here," or some other such statement implying that the giving of recognition was a rare occurrence.

Salary is cited as frequently for giving rise to negative as to positive feelings about the job. We shall continue to postpone discussion of salary until we have presented some additional findings.

In 14 per cent of the stories the factor of work itself was mentioned as being involved in the negative job attitudes of the respondents. An example of this is the story told by a young design draftsman. He reported on a time when he was assigned nothing but tables and side arms to design because he had shown he could do these satisfactorily. He had no chance to use his creative ability, and his opportunities to learn and expand his scope were minimal. He felt he had become nothing more than a number to the company. His work became sloppy, and he began to receive change slips because of errors in the construction of machinery he had designed. He finally had to leave the company for a new job because he was bothered by the poor work he was turning out.

Two other factors occurred in at least 10 per cent of the low-attitude stories: advancement and working conditions. Like company policy and administration, working conditions are mentioned to any extent only in the low sequences of events. Paramount in the complaints about working conditions were inconvenience of the location of the plant, the inadequacy of facilities to do the job, and the amount of work required on the job. *Workers complained of too little work more than of too much.*

Failure to get an anticipated advancement described most of the situations in which advancement was coded in a low sequence. The expectations of the employee seemed to play a crucial role in determining the job attitude effects of promotions. We have seen previously that in about half the stories in which an advancement led to an increase in job satisfaction the advancement came unexpectedly.

1. Long-range versus short-range attitude changes. The overall frequency of short-term attitude sequences is larger than the equivalent group in the highs. With the lows, failure to obtain recognition is the key factor in sequences in which the feelings do not persist beyond the short time span covered by the incident. Just as with the highs, recognition seems to play a role only as a partial reinforcer of job attitudes (cf. Table 6).

2. *Interrelationship of factors.* Let us now examine the interrelationships of the factors as they appeared in the stories of both high and low job attitudes. Table 7 presents the frequency with which the major factors appeared with other factors in the stories that we were told. The factors that appeared together infrequently are not shown. We shall re-examine those satisfying factors that showed substantial frequency in the low sequences of events.

When failure to receive recognition was coded in a low sequence of events, it was most often the only factor present in the situation. Next in order of frequency, it appeared with a description of some ineffective company policy or administrative

TABLE 7

Interrelationships among First-Level Factors in the Lows *

Recognition	with	company policy and administration	22%
Possibility of growth	with	company policy and administration	38
Advancement	with	company policy and administration	39
Salary	with	company policy and administration	51
Interpersonal relationships—supervisors	with	supervision-technical	50
Interpersonal relationships—peers	with	company policy and administration	21
Supervision-technical	with	interpersonal relationship—supervisor	38
Company policy and administration	with	salary	28
Working conditions	with	company policy and administration	30
Work itself	with	company policy and administration	29

* This table gives the percentage frequency with which the factors on the left occurred in sequences in which the factors on the right were also found.

act; whereas, as previously stated, in the high sequences of events it was most commonly related to an act of achievement. This difference suggests two things. First, that the simple failure to receive recognition can be a source for job dissatisfaction. Second, that in many of the situations in which there has been a failure to give recognition another major ingredient is the company policy and administrative practices. The nature of the failure to give recognition is often qualitatively different in the low stories than the nature of recognition that appears in the high job-attitude stories. In the highs it is generally related to the successful completion of a task, whereas in the lows it is a reflection of a job situation as affected by poor company policies or administrative practices.

Again we see this same qualitative difference for the factor of advancement. Advancement generally occurs in high stories in which a description of the interesting nature of the work is given, whereas in the lows it appears most often in stories again describing poor company policies or administrative practices. The same difference in association is true of the factor of work itself. In the highs work itself appears in stories describing achievements and responsibilities; in the lows, in conjunction with poor company policies and administration. From this analysis of the interrelationship of the factors, as they appeared in the stories, it would seem that much of the time when the satisfying factors are contributory to poor job attitudes they occur in situations describing the job context rather than the elements of the work and its rewarding qualities.

3. Second-level factors. In contrast with the highs, the most frequent second-level factor appearing in the low stories is feelings of unfairness (cf. Table 8). The individual became unhappy on the job because he perceived what had happened as an indication of a lack of concern that his superiors or the company in general had for him as an individual. Often this was a feeling that the company lacked integrity. A close second, but of more importance because of their relationship to long-range attitude changes, were feelings of block to growth. The individual interpreted the events as meaning that he was not getting anywhere on his job. The events were a definite signal to him that his job aspirations would not be achieved.

The second-level factors of recognition and achievement again

TABLE 8

Percentage of Each Second-Level Factor Appearing in High and Low Job-Attitude Sequences

Duration of Feelings

	High			Low		
	Long *	Short	Total	Long *	Short	Total
1. Recognition	57	64	59 †	27	24	26
2. Achievement	57	56	57 †	18	24	19
3. Possible growth	42	18	38	43	7	33
4. Advancement	3	3	3	2	1	2
5. Responsibility	33	18	30 †	9	7	8
6. Group feeling	11	8	10 †	3	4	3
7. Work itself	33	8	29 †	16	4	13
8. Status	21	5	18	10	10	10
9. Security	7	5	7	11	6	9
10. Fairness-unfairness	2	5	3	35	44	38
11. Pride, guilt, inadequacy	9	10	9	14	15	14
12. Salary	22	5	19	18	1	13

* This column includes the frequency of lasting attitudes resulting from both long-range and short-range sequences.

† Difference in totals statistically significant at .01 level of confidence.

appear in about one fifth to one fourth of the low-attitude stories. This is less than half as frequent as in the high stories.

It should be noted that for the second-level factors there is also a greater variability in the percentage values within the high stories than in the low sequences, a difference again statistically significant. Inasmuch as feelings of unfairness were the most frequently expressed by our respondents for their negative job-attitude reaction, this difference in variability between highs and lows is understandable, since any factor can be perceived as being unfair.

4. Interrelationship of second-level factors. If we compare the interrelationships of the factors in the high stories and in the low job-attitude stories shown in Table 9, we again see the qualitative difference between the factors when they appear in the highs as opposed to when they appear in the lows. Recognition in the high stories is associated with feelings of possible growth and achievement; in the low stories it is most frequently associated with feelings of unfairness. Possible growth also shows an association with recognition and achievement in the

TABLE 9

Relationship of Each Second-Level Factor to Other Second-Level Factors *

| | | | Percentage | |
			High	Low
Recognition	with	achievement	37	
		possibility of growth	39	
		fairness-unfairness		41
Possible growth	with	recognition	63	
		achievement	37	
		fairness-unfairness		35
Salary	with	recognition	77	
		possible growth	66	36
		responsibility	43	
		fairness-unfairness		61

* This table gives the percentage frequency with which the factors on the left occurred in sequences in which the factors on the right were also found.

high stories, whereas in the low stories it accompanies feelings of being treated unfairly by the company or the supervisor. It should be noted that the factor of fairness-unfairness appears extremely infrequently in the high-sequence stories.

The results at the feeling level pretty much parallel the results that were found for the first-level factors. They serve to emphasize the importance of professional growth as the key want of employees and as the basic determiner of positive job attitudes. They also explain why the job context factors are involved in bringing about job dissatisfaction. These are the factors that can serve to treat the employee unfairly, unfair, of course, in terms of his own perceptions. We have more to say on this point in the next section.

High versus Low Job-Attitude Sequences

When we contrast the results from the low sequences of events with those from the high sequences, several major differences become apparent.

For the lows, the range of percentages among the sixteen factors is not so large as for the highs. Five of the factors in the high sequences appeared in as many as one fifth of the stories. In contrast to this, only two factors in the low sequences appeared that often. On the other hand, six factors in the low sequences have percentages between 10 and 19 per cent, and only one factor in the high sequences was in that range. For the highs, as we have seen before, there are a few factors that stand out as satisfiers, with the remaining factors making a negligible contribution to job satisfaction. For the lows, the differences in the percentages among the factors is small in contrast. The greater variability of percentages for the high sequences is statistically significant. From this result we can speculate that the factors included in this study show more equal potentiality for leading to job dissatisfaction than they do for leading to job satisfaction. A great many things evidently can be the source of dissatisfaction, whereas only those factors that we mentioned previously can contribute to bringing about positive job attitudes. We shall shortly suggest an explanation for the more equal appearance of the factors in the low job-attitude stories.

Table 6 presents the data with which we can test the basic hypothesis we postulated at the beginning of this chapter. We said that there were certain factors that would operate only to increase job satisfaction and that there would be other factors with the power only to decrease job satisfaction. There is good support in the data for this concept. The factors of greatest frequency in the low sequences of events, company policy and administration and supervision (both technical and human relations), rarely appeared in the high stories. With salary again an exception, for every factor that appeared more frequently in the lows than in the highs there was a negligible frequency in the high sequences. This was true for the interpersonal relationships with peers, working conditions, and the factor of personal life, as well as for company policy and administration and the two supervision factors.

The results for the high sequences of events also give basic substantiation to the hypothesis with one qualifying modification. All the basic satisfiers, *recognition, achievement, advancement, responsibility,* and *work itself,* appeared with significantly greater frequencies in the highs than they did in the low sequences of events. However, some of these factors also appeared with some frequency in the low stories: recognition, 18 per cent; work itself, 14 per cent; and advancement, 11 per cent. Evidently these three satisfiers are not so unidirectional in their effect on job attitudes as the factors that cause job dissatisfaction. From these results it would appear that a better statement of the hypothesis would be that the satisfier factors are much more likely to increase job satisfaction than they would be to decrease job satisfaction but that the factors that relate to job dissatisfaction very infrequently act to increase job satisfaction. However, two of the satisfiers operate substantially in a unidirectional manner. Achievement, which is the most frequently occurring factor in the high job-attitude stories, and responsibility appeared in only 7 and 6 per cent, respectively, of the low job-attitude stories.

Figure 1 shows the results of this basic hypothesis, the distinction between satisfiers and dissatisfiers, as it turned out from the results of our study. As indicated in the legend of this figure, the distance from the neutral area shows the percentage frequency with which each factor occurred in the high job-attitude sequences and in the low job-attitude sequences. The width

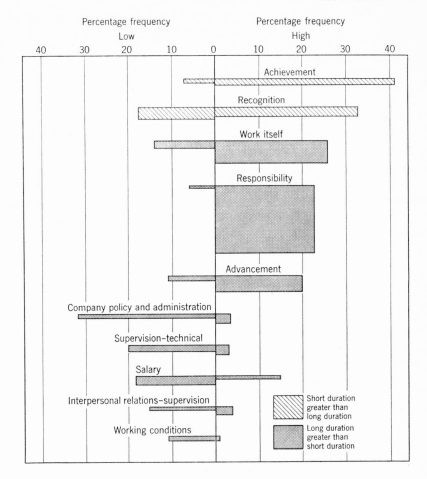

Figure 1. *Comparison of satisfiers and dissatisfiers*

of the boxes represents the ratio of long-range to short-range attitude effects; the wider the box, the more frequently this factor led to a long-range job attitude change. The factors of recognition and achievement are shaded in this figure to indicate that the width of their boxes portrays a reversal in the long-range ratio. The attitude effects of both of these factors were substantially more short-range.

Considering both frequency and duration of attitude effects, the three factors of work itself, responsibility, and advancement stand out strongly as the major factors involved in producing high job attitudes. Their role in producing poor job attitudes is by contrast extremely small. Contrariwise, company policy and administration, supervision (both technical and interpersonal relationships), and working conditions represent the major job dissatisfiers with little potency to affect job attitudes in a positive direction.

The differences shown in Figure 1 indicate another very basic distinction between the factors found in high job attitudes and those found in the stories about low job attitudes. We have previously said that all the motivating factors focused on the job and that the factors that appeared infrequently in the high job-attitude stories could be characterized as describing the job context. It is just these job context factors, company policy and administration, supervision (technical and human relations), and working conditions, that now appear as the job dissatisfiers. We can expand on the previous hypothesis by stating that the job satisfiers deal with the factors involved in doing the job, whereas the job dissatisfiers deal with the factors that define the job context. Poor working conditions, bad company policies and administration, and bad supervision will lead to job dissatisfaction. Good company policies, good administration, good supervision, and good working conditions will not lead to positive job attitudes. In opposition to this, as far as our data has gone, recognition, achievement, interesting work, responsibility, and advancement all lead to positive job attitudes. Their absence will much less frequently lead to job dissatisfaction.

Salary

We are now ready to examine the factor of salary. It appears as frequently in the high sequences as it does in the low sequences. This is true, however, only when we compare totals, combining short- and long-range attitude changes. If we examine Table 6 for duration of attitude change, we find that in the lows salary is found almost three times as often in the long-range as in the short-range sequences. For the high job-attitude stories salary is about equal in both durations. It would seem that as an affector of job attitudes salary has more potency as a job dissatisfier than as a job satisfier.

Returning to the interrelationship of the factors in Tables 7 and 9, we can see that salary was associated with company policy and administration in about one half of the low sequences of events; in the high sequences it was most frequently associated with advancement and work itself. To be more specific, when salary occurred as a factor in the lows, it revolved around the unfairness (cf. Table 9) of the wage system within the company, and this almost always referred to increases in salaries rather than the absolute levels. It was the system of salary administration that was being described, a system in which wage increases were obtained grudgingly, or given too late, or in which the differentials between newly hired employees and those with years of experience on the job were too small. Occasionally, it concerned an advancement that was not accompanied by a salary increase. In contrast to this, salary was mentioned in the high stories as something that went along with a person's achievement on the job. It was a form of recognition; it meant more than money; it meant a job well done; it meant that the individual was progressing in his work. Viewed within the context of the sequences of events, salary as a factor belongs more in the group that defines the job situation and is primarily a dissatisfier.

Chapter 9   The Effects

The methodological sections of this book should have given some indication of the limitations attached to subjective data on the effects of job attitudes. We recognize the likelihood that many readers will be skeptical of the validity of our respondents' reports that given behaviors were consequent upon their feelings about their jobs. However, as we have indicated before (see page 16), the lack of meaningful objective criteria makes it essential that we use what cues we have to the impact of people's attitudes on the way in which they behave in the work situation.

A further problem with our technique, which has been discussed at some length, was the necessity for indicating in some detail to the respondents the kinds of behavior we wanted them to talk about. It would clearly have been more elegant methodologically to leave completely open the question of the effects and their nature. However, we discovered early in our pilot procedure that the respondents themselves wished some guidance as to the kind of material in which we were interested. Let us then present our data on effects in full knowledge of the fact that they were elicited by specific probes directed toward the kind of behavior with which we were concerned and that, therefore, they should not be considered direct evidence of the behavior of our respondents but rather indications that this behavior had a high degree of probability and that observation or other objective measures of behavior would be likely to yield the same results. The precise nature of the probes we used can be seen in Appendix I.

The discussion on effects follows the general outline of the categories in our content analysis (see Appendix II). These categories are *performance, turnover, mental health, interpersonal relations,* and *attitudinal effects.*

Performance Effects

The nature of performance effects described in our study deserves some special mention. It is clear that we have no quantitative measure of changes in output, such as are available in many studies in industry. What we have is the respondent's report of a change in the performance of his work, accompanied, for many, by a fairly precise and circumstantial account of the way in which this effect on productivity was perceived. Thus, we cannot compare any given instance of change with any other with respect to the *amount* of effect. However, we can count the frequency with which people report such changes in their work patterns.

Here are a few of the statements made concerning the effects of attitudes upon performance:

> When I realized I wasn't getting anywhere with my supervisor, I quit trying. You know what I mean. I put out the work all right, but I didn't bother with all those little finishing touches which are the difference between a good drawing and one that is only so-so. Also, I never bothered hurrying. When things got done they got done.

> After they put me in charge of the project, and I felt that I had a job that was all my own, everything seemed to click. You know how it is when you are hot. Problems you could stay at for days almost seem to solve themselves. I don't think I ever did a better piece of work in my life.

And more briefly:

> The lift that I got led (me to work) fourteen hours a day, six days a week—had the drive to work those hours.

> I dived into work with much more enthusiasm.

> I worked harder and put more ego into my work . . . took work home to do on my own time . . . eager to come back next day and plug a little more.

> First couple days I didn't carry my share of the burden, just thinking about the thing that happened . . . put a lot of work off.

> Just stared out of the window all day with my arms folded . . . I just didn't work at all.

> Not working up to capacity.

Note the wide range of variability implied. There seemed to be an assumed level of standard performance. When lowered productivity was reported, the level was clearly below this stand-

TABLE 10

Percentage of Performance Effects

	High	Low
Long range	79	51
Short range	44	41
Total	73	48

ard.   When improvement in performance was reported, productivity was not merely at standard levels but considerably above and beyond them.   The effects reported were very real and in no sense inconsequential.

The statements varied in specificity—in some instances the respondents could describe a specific task they had performed better or worse or were able to make statements about the amount of time devoted to their jobs or to the rate at which they worked.   Elsewhere, no specific example was given—the respondent indicated that the effect was all pervasive, that, for example, he had felt that his total job was performed in a more creative or more inspired manner.

Table 10 indicates the frequency with which these effects were reported in both long-range and short-range sequences in highs and lows.   Note that almost three out of four high sequences involved an improvement in performance as a result of an improved attitude on the job.   Note also the difference between long-range and short-range sequences in this group.*   A higher percentage of long-range than short-range sequences have performance effects.   Those attitudes which are more lasting have a greater tendency to affect performance than momentary attitude changes.

About one half of the low sequences included performance effects.   This, too, is a substantial proportion, although it is significantly lower than the one for high sequences.

Two findings emerge, then, from the data concerning performance effects.   According to the people we interviewed, attitudes toward the job exerted an extremely important influence on the

---

* All differences mentioned in text on effects are statistically significant at the .01 level of confidence or better.

way in which the job was done. In over 60 per cent of the combined high and low sequences an effect on performance was reported in the anticipated direction; that is, an improved performance related to improved job attitudes and a decrease in performance related to a change of attitude in a negative direction. The second finding is that the tendency for attitudes to have an effect on performance was greater for favorable attitudes toward the job than for unfavorable ones. An unknown part of the difference between the 73 per cent reported effects of high sequences and 48 per cent reported effects of low sequences may be attributed to the unwillingness of some interviewees to admit to doing their jobs less well than usual.

It has certainly occurred to the reader that it would be more painful to people to report of themselves that their work was poor or inefficient than that it had improved in quality. We have no way of knowing to what extent the remarkable difference in the frequency of performance effects between high and low sequences is due to such psychological screening. Here again, we know what *was* reported; we do not know what was suppressed. However, it is important to note that the difference in the frequency of reports of performance effects in the lows and highs is consistent with the general pattern of lows and highs. The highs do revolve more about the job and the way it is done; the lows do revolve around factors extrinsic to the job. We should recognize the fact that in a certain proportion of the lows the central factors were related to the jobs, and there were effects on work performance. However, this pattern remains far more characteristic for the highs.

There is one finding in the literature that is consistent with our results. The contradictory nature of the relationship between morale and productivity has been noted frequently. It is possible that such contradictory relationships stem from the fact that the usual morale measures are confounded because they tap both the kinds of attitudes that we find in our highs and those we find in our lows. If this were so, the degree of relationship between morale and productivity would be more dependent upon that component of morale related to highs than that related to lows in any given study because of the greater potency of the highs for productivity change.

Even with ideal measures of effects, a positive relationship between morale and productivity would come from that part of the morale measure that depended on satisfiers. If the proportion of positive attitude-effect relationships were low, the overall result could easily approach randomness. In any event, the frequently found low correlations between morale and productivity are not inconsistent with our findings, which were obtained through a technique so different from the correlational approach.

Turnover

After I saw the least competent man promoted because he was friendly with the chief I was through. I wasn't up for promotion myself, but I didn't have the feeling I would get a fair shake when I would be. The first chance I had several months later I resigned and left for a new job.

First reaction—thought of leaving.

Thought about leaving constantly . . . was almost forced to leave many times.

Definitely got to the point where I would just as soon have left. Problem was where to go. Had made a start . . .

In addition to those who actually quit as a result of negative attitudes, many of our respondents reported reactions such as those quoted—they thought about quitting or actually took steps to leave; that is, they read ads or had interviews with other companies or with employment agencies. The import of such psychological leaving of the company should not be minimized.

Those who gave turnover information as an effect of high sequences indicated that as a result of a positive attitude toward the job they had either changed their minds about a previous decision to quit or had turned down an offer from another company.

As shown in Table 11, about one out of eight low sequences resulted in quits. Note that within the group of lows the frequency is higher for long-range than for short-range sequences. Thus it was rare that a short-range sequence led to quitting, but the proportion of reported quits as a result of long-range low sequences is considerable.

In addition to those who actually quit, another 8 per cent of the respondents who reported low sequences indicated that they took steps toward quitting. This was true for over one tenth of the long-range lows. In an additional 20 per cent of the long-

TABLE 11

Percentage of Turnover Effects

	High		Low	
	Would Not Now	Quit	Took Steps	Thought of
Long range	11	17	11	20
Short range	0	3	1	8
Total	9	13	8	17

range low sequences individuals thought about quitting. Thus almost half of the long-range low sequences resulted in some degree of physical or psychological withdrawal from the job. The implications to industry are apparent. The price of such withdrawal cannot be computed in money. Can one add up the cost of such a great amount of turnover, the difficulty of obtaining personnel, and the losses to industry of having on the staff people who have quit the company psychologically?

It is impossible to evaluate the effect of positive job attitudes in increasing the psychological commitment of an individual to his job. We were told of this effect in about one tenth of the high sequences, but the point only came up for those who had had an attractive offer of another job or a previous feeling of discontent leading to a decision to quit.

These findings relating job attitudes to turnover fit in well with the studies that describe a similar relationship report in Chapter IV of *Job Attitudes: Review of Research and Opinion* (23). Most of the studies reported in that chapter were based on respondents at the rank-and-file level. The information obtained from our sample corroborates the belief that such a relationship exists at the professional-managerial level as well.

Attitude Toward the Company

The one remaining effect that relates to the company in an obvious way is the attitude of the individual toward the company. Our respondents were asked to indicate whether or not

TABLE 12

Percentage of Changes in Attitude Toward the Company

	High	Low
	Positive Change	Negative Change
Long range	48	34
Short range	31	11
Total	45	27

feelings engendered by the sequence of events affected their over-all attitude toward the company.

As shown in Table 12, almost half of the respondents said, in discussing their highs, that one result was a more favorable attitude toward the company as a whole. Slightly over one fourth claimed that low job attitudes led to a lower regard for the company as a place to work.

The percentage is sizable in both groups; a company may expect the degree of loyalty it gets from its employees to vary with the degree of their job satisfaction. As with performance effects, the relationship between job attitude and attitude toward the company is stronger in highs than in lows. This is a particularly striking result, in view of the large number of low sequences that revolved around company policies. Here, too, then, the data support the belief that job attitudes are potent and that positive attitudes are more potent than negative ones.

Mental-Health Effects

The kinds of reports that were coded as mental-health effects were of many varieties. The one common thread was that they reflected a deleterious effect on the well-being of the worker. In most reports of mental-health effects these phenomena were obviously short-lived and not of the kind usually associated with mental illness. Thus headaches, loss of appetite, and attacks of indigestion or nausea are hardly signs of neurosis or psychosis. Even the very small number of real illnesses reported were not necessarily entirely psychogenic. However, in every instance the difficulty was ascribed by the respondent to tensions over his job, as with the sufferer from angina for whom a run-in with his supervisor inevitably brought on an attack.

Two points should be made before discussing what we have classified as mental-health effects. First, a point of terminology. "Depression" and "elation" are terms used in psychiatric literature which connote disturbances in affect and are often associated with neurotic states. These terms were often given by our respondents in discussing high and low sequences. Most of these reports were unaccompanied by the usual symptoms indicating psychiatric disturbance. Therefore, except in those instances in which other evidences of maladjustment were reported, we did not code an unamplified statement of elation or depression as a mental-health effect. We considered these reports as descriptive of the total pattern of positive or negative attitudes toward the job.

Second, in assessing the over-all importance of mental-health effects from these data we must not forget that we are dealing, on the whole, with a group of successful men. The casualties of the industrial world did not appear in our sample. By the definition of this sample, all of our respondents had been able to maintain a sufficiently adequate adjustment to remain within the ranks of managerial-professional personnel. It is, therefore, impressive to see what a wide range of deleterious effects on adjustment were traced by these people to the events that occurred during periods of low job attitudes.

> I have angina. Every time I have a run-in with my supervisor I get an attack. Then I take my medicine and I get over it. I

TABLE 13

Percentage of Mental-Health Effects

| | High | Low | |
	Improvement	Psychosomatic	Tension Symptoms
Long range	14	5	23
Short range	0	3	19
Total	12	4	23

ought to quit now but I am only four years from retirement. Where could I go?

When I came back and found that my chief had gone over my head in dealing with my section without telling me I realized I was on the skids here. I started drinking and smoking too much. Never had an auto accident before but I banged up my fenders twice during that month. I must have lost twenty pounds.

It is obvious that we have no objective and conclusive evidence that these symptoms were caused by the job attitudes. It is difficult indeed to imagine an experimental design that would show causation for functional illness. But it is clear, at least, that these people perceived a relationship; they believed their illness to be related to attitudes on the job. And it is not inconsistent with medical and psychological knowledge and theory that there was good reason for their belief.

In 12 per cent of the high sequences respondents reported improvement in mental-health symptoms. "Slept better and ate better as a result." "Coming with general feeling of satisfaction get better eating, working, and sleeping habits. Previous dissatisfaction had led to nervousness and inability to relax." As with turnover, this 12 per cent is an underestimate. The individual would have had to have some mental-health symptom before he could have reported improvement. Therefore, we cannot assess fully the positive effects on psychological adjustment from improved job attitudes.

Industry has evidenced considerable interest in the mental health of its employees. Here, then, is another sphere with which management has been concerned and in which job attitudes apparently play a decided role.

Interpersonal Relationship as Effects

Managerial and professional people notoriously take their jobs home with them. As Table 14 shows, about one quarter of our stories included as a component of the effects of job attitudes some noticeable change in interpersonal relationships. The largest part of these changes consisted of the improvement or deterioration of home life. Actually, it may be somewhat surprising that so small a proportion of the stories included such a report. After all, we did ask a specifically leading question in

TABLE 14

Percentage of Interpersonal Relationship Effects

	High	Low
Long range	30	28
Short range	18	24
Total	28	27

this area (cf. Appendix I). Many of our respondents very pointedly informed us that they did *not* let the tensions of the job affect their families. Is this a sign of the psychological sturdiness of our sample? Perhaps we should have asked their wives.

Somewhat more surprising, and of considerable moment to the thesis presented in Part III of this book, is the relatively small frequency with which a circumstantial account was given of effects from positive or negative job attitudes on interpersonal relationships at work. We did not code this category, incidentally, for *casual* assents to our query as to whether improved or deteriorated interpersonal relationships on the job were a part of the sequence of events.

Two more points can be made from Table 14. First, there is little difference in the frequency of effects on interpersonal relationships between the highs and the lows. It is likely that the degree to which a person lets his feelings about his job spill over into the conduct of his interpersonal relationships is more a function of his psychological dynamics as an individual than of anything else.

Second, there is a consistent, but not significant, tendency for long-range sequences to include effects on interpersonal relationships more frequently than short-range sequences. This increased frequency in long-range tendencies is significantly more marked for high than for low sequences.

Attitudinal Effects

Table 15 summarizes our information about attitudinal effects. This rounds out our picture of the consequences of job attitudes.

TABLE 15

Percentage of Attitudinal Effects

Attitude Toward	High	Low
Individual	6	27
Company	45	27
Profession	17	11
Security	7	5
Confidence	26	4
Total (1 or more)	71	56

Beyond the specific feelings about the job, which were the central theme of each sequence of events, there were many other changes in attitudes. We elicited some of the information on which we based our descriptions of these changes when we explored the criticalness of the sequence (cf. Chapter 2). Other information was given spontaneously by the respondent or emerged during answers to questions directed towards factors or behavioral effects.

There is a significant difference (see Table 15) between the kinds of attitudinal effects manifested in the highs and those in the lows. In the highs the beneficial results of positive feelings about the job are extended to the person's attitudes toward the company, and, even more striking, toward increased self-confidence. These attitudinal effects, along with the increase of positive feeling about the profession, are much more noticeable in the long-range than in the short-range sequences.

For the low sequences the attitudinal effects are referred away from the person himself. In view of the importance of the second-level factor of reactions to others, it is consistent that one of the commoner motifs among the lows should be a change in attitude toward a specific individual, usually a supervisor.

Again, as with performance effects, we can compare the potency of satisfaction and dissatisfaction. This is in contrast to the turnover and mental-health areas in which the very nature of the effects makes it unlikely that they would be equally represented in highs and lows. The evidence in Table 15 reinforces the conclusion drawn from the analysis of performance effects that high morale is more potent in producing effects than low morale. The sheer number of attitudinal effects is significantly greater in the highs. This comparison was made by contrasting the number of sequences in each group in which one or more attitudinal effects could be coded. Among the individual attitudinal effects only a changed attitude toward an individual is more frequent in the lows. Moreover, even though there is a statistically significant tendency for attitudinal effects to occur more frequently in the long-range than in the short-range sequences, the size of this difference is significantly greater among the lows than among the highs. This argues that attitudinal effects are less likely to occur in a low, unless the sequence of events covers a long time span; although this difference *does* occur for the highs, the chance that a short-range high will lead to lasting changes in many attitudes is great. Note that this extends our previous finding that for the highs the specific attitude toward the job is also likely to persist beyond the immediate time span of an incident.

Effects as Related to Factors and to Demographic Variables

A further hypothesis we tested with regard to effects was twofold—that effects would vary with the factors causing the attitudes and also with the characteristics of the individual. On both counts this hypothesis must be rejected. With the two exceptions of responsibility and work itself, which were mentioned in the preceding section, there was essentially no difference in proportion of effects produced by various factors. It is a basic finding of the study that factors are not equally likely to produce a high or low attitude—but if an attitude is produced by any factor it is just as likely to produce an effect as an attitude caused by any other factor.

Similarly, there were few differences in effects, as reported by various categories of individuals; that is, engineers versus accountants, various age breakdowns, job-level categories, etc. The few differences that appeared are merely suggestive and are discussed in the next section. With few exceptions, we may say that effects appeared in approximately equal proportions for all categories of individuals interviewed.

These are important findings. They suggest that attitudes are a potent force for all individuals in our sample under all sets of conditions.

Summary

To recapitulate the data discussed in this chapter, we can make two statements. First, job attitudes are a powerful force and are functionally related to the productivity, stability, and adjustment of the industrial working force. Second, the differences between satisfiers and dissatisfiers developed in the preceding chapter involve not only a qualitative difference in factors but a difference, largely quantitative, in effects. Specifically, the positive effects of high attitudes are more potent than the negative effects of low attitudes.

Chapter 10   Individuals

Any analysis of the distribution of factors or effects among different categories of individuals in a sample of the size studied in this experiment would of necessity have to be handled with extreme caution. Although our sample was not unduly small for the purposes of an inductive study of this kind, it is true that analyses along demographic lines are limited by the size of the sample. Thus, although it is perfectly practical to divide our sample along individual dimensions, such as age, occupational status, level in a hierarchy, or education, the numbers in individual groups become vanishingly small when an attempt is made to "cross-break" along the lines of more than one variable at a time. For example, although it would be possible to compare engineers and accountants, an attempt to compare young engineers with young accountants, especially if we were also to introduce the factor of educational level, would reduce the size of the sample in individual categories to an impractically small number. However, as long as our analyses are confined to the treatment of these variables one at a time and as long as we are aware of the fact that any conclusions to which these analyses lead us are highly tentative, we can investigate the way in which individual characteristics of our respondents are related to the sequences of events they report.

Differences in the Lows

The first finding that emerges from such an analysis is somewhat startling. We compared the frequency with which any of the first- or second-level factors or effects occur in groups differing with respect to our major demographic variables. It turned out that there were virtually no significant differences for the lows. That is, it did not matter whether a man was an accountant, old or young, educated or uneducated, or in a high-level or a low-level job. The same kinds of objective situations led to low morale among all our respondents; they led to the same effects. The second-level factors also appeared in approximately the same proportion among the different kinds of people in our sample. This reinforces the notion presented earlier in this report that there is a kind of equipotentiality in the degree to which the different "dissatisfiers" will lead to bad morale.

Actually, there are some differences in these lows, even if there are not enough of them among the large number of potential differences to lead to any firm conclusions. The few differences there are seem to be clearly explicable in situational terms. Thus younger and college-trained men more frequently mentioned the characteristics of the work itself as a reason for feeling bad than the older and noncollege-trained men in our sample. It is likely that both the younger and the college-trained men were upwardly mobile. We might expect them to be sensitive to tedious and unfulfilling jobs.

Of somewhat greater consequence is the fact that we did not find any serious tendency within any of the groups to emphasize other job-related factors to a greater or lesser extent in lows, nor did we find serious differences in the frequencies with which characteristics of interpersonal relationships or other "contextual" factors were responsible for highs. Apparently, anyone in almost any situation can run into trouble with his relationships with other people or can react negatively to company atmosphere and company policy and thus develop a period of low morale.

Factors among the Highs

There are five significant differences in frequency of occurrence of first-level factors as a function of our demographic analyses. The first four of these hold together in a rather interesting pattern, which is reminiscent of some of the findings from morale surveys cited in *Job Attitudes: Review of Research and Opinion* (23). Recognition was cited more frequently by individuals of high than those of lower educational level. Among individuals high in the hierarchy of industry both recognition and achievement were more frequently cited than among low-level individuals. Lastly, among individuals who were in the older age brackets achievement was more frequently cited than among younger people. Although level and age may very well be related, it is probable that education and age are inversely related, if at all. Thus, we have at least two probable independent divisions that demonstrate a greater frequency with which certain of the satisfiers were cited. Note that these analyses refer to age and status at the time of the sequence.

In Chapter II of *Job Attitudes: Review of Research and Opinion* (23) the collation of many demographic studies of morale shows that the highest morale was found in older age groups, in groups who were high in occupational level, and, to a lesser extent, in groups high in education. It seems interesting that the groups found to rank high in morale surveys should also mention more frequently the job-related factors identified in our techniques.

Has this finding any explanation? There are two possibilities. The first is that this group was objectively in a situation in which satisfiers were present to a greater degree than is true for the rest of the population. They were in more responsible jobs, in jobs which have greater skill requirements, and they themselves were more called upon for unusual accomplishments than is true for the average working man. Another possibility is that the actual frequency of the satisfiers may not be greater or less in these people's jobs than in others' but that it is a characteristic of these people to react to satisfiers more vigorously than would the run of the population. It is probable that the most responsible, most creative, and brightest people would be found in this group high in education, status, and in their most vigorous and creative years.

It is our feeling that both explanations have some merit. That is, undoubtedly throughout the range of occupations and situations it is likely that there are objective differences in the degree to which intrinsically satisfying conditions related to the job are possible. Within the sample chosen for this study all of the individuals were in jobs that by definition showed some possibility of individual creative work. Thus it should have been possible for almost everyone to tell us about a situation involving a satisfier. In fact, almost everyone did. Despite the fact that a given part of our sample, which in studies different from our own shows higher morale than average, gave us *more* material related to satisfiers, there is probably also an individual component. Future research studies should investigate the degree to which this individual component, as contrasted with situational components, determines the occurrence of high morale and its consequent effects.

Engineers and Accountants

A study of Table 16 indicates that we have established, in a tentative way at least, similarity in findings for our two professional samples. Note particularly the total lack of significant differences among the lows. The kinds of situations that produce periods of low morale are equally possible and equally obnoxious both to engineers and to accountants.

There are some differences in the highs. These differences, however, do not reflect on our major thesis. If, for example, we had found a greater tendency for engineers or accountants to report extrinsic factors in their highs or job-related factors in the lows, then we would have had reason to doubt the generality of our findings. However, the differences are in the degree of emphasis among different aspects of the satisfiers that play so important a role in producing periods of positive attitudes toward a job.

The pattern of these differences suggests that situational factors are probably responsible. Thus we can note that among the engineers we have significantly higher frequency of entries under responsibility; among accountants we have significantly higher frequency of entries under advancement. It is likely that in the hierarchical world of accounting any increase in job responsibility would be accompanied by a change in status. We notice, for example, that there is actually a greater frequency of second-level possible growth among accountants than engineers. This difference is of borderline significance. Among engineers, especially among the group studied in this sample, fixity of the hierarchy is somewhat less marked. Thus we received a fairly good number of stories in which individuals were given new responsibilities without an accompanying change in formal status. A design engineer would report the excitement of being asked

TABLE 16

Comparison of Engineers and Accountants

	Highs		Lows	
	Engineers	Accountants	Engineers	Accountants
First-Level Factors:				
Recognition	33	34	19	17
Achievement	43	38	10	4
Possible growth	3	9	10	6
Advancement	14	27 *	9	15
Salary	15	15	18	16
Interpersonal relationships—superior	5	3	13	18
Interpersonal relationships—subordinate	5	6	1	5
Interpersonal relationships—peers	2	4	10	5
Supervision-technical	3	2	22	18
Responsibility	28	17 †	4	7
Company policy and administration	3	2	27	37
Working conditions	2	0	9	13
Work itself	33	17 †	14	15
Personal life	2	0	5	7
Status	5	4	3	6
Job security	0	1	1	2
Second-Level Factors:				
Recognition	54	64	24	27
Achievement	58	54	21	17
Possible growth	33	49 *	32	35
Advancement	4	1	2	2
Responsibility	35	25	6	11
Group feeling	8	12	4	2
Work itself	37	18 †	13	12
Status	18	18	9	12
Security	6	8	6	13
Reactions	4	1	40	35
Pride, guilt, inadequacy	14	3	17	10
Salary	15	25	13	14

* Difference between Engineers and Accountants significant at .05 level of confidence.

† Difference between Engineers and Accountants significant at .01 level of confidence.

to supervise the creation of a complete new machine instead of his usual task of working on small parts. This is a kind of added responsibility without any formal change in status. It is harder to conceive of such happenings within the more structured world of accountants.

Another difference that is probably situationally determined is the rather consistent pattern in which engineers give more frequent notice than accountants to the actual conduct of work itself. The second-level factor of interest in the work and also performance effects are more frequent among engineers. Most of us would agree that the day-to-day job of the engineer is probably more fascinating than the day-to-day job of an accountant even at a high professional level. That this is reflected in the reports that engineers give of times when they feel good about their jobs is hardly surprising. As indicated in a later discussion, the interest in the doing of the job, although it is a component of basic motivation for work, is not necessarily the most significant one. The fact that on an over-all basis accountants with somewhat less interesting jobs do not show a lower frequency of intrinsic factors in their highs argues that motivation is related to a more fundamental psychological process than that based primarily on the interest of the job.

A Final Note

In summary, it is our feeling that the general lack of individual differences in the occurrence of factors and effects argues the applicability of our findings beyond the immediate bounds of the small sample with which we worked. We recognize the fact that this is an inference and no more. The hypotheses advanced in this book need to be tested with larger samples of individuals and over a much broader spectrum of educational and occupational backgrounds. We recognize also that the individual differences that would emerge under these circumstances would very probably reflect themselves to a greater extent in the findings than was true in our own limited sample. For example, it is very likely that a procedure patterned after ours, if applied to routine assembly-line workers, would yield relatively little data of the kind we found in our highs primarily because of the low degree to which such factors are possible within these jobs. It is our suspicion that the quality of the lows would not change very much from level to level or within various educational groups.

One further thought has occurred on the basis of our examination of the data. It may be that there are individuals who because of their training and because of the things that have happened to them have learned to react positively to the factors associated with the context of their jobs. We find some evidence of the existence of these individuals in the small number of stories among the highs that were concerned with these contextual factors. One of the objectives of research with a wider range of occupational groups might be to note the characteristics of people who present interpersonal relations and other extrinsic factors as sources for periods of highly positive attitudes towards their jobs. Certainly, with different kinds of populations, salesmen, for example, or production supervisors, one would expect a greater frequency in such categories from the nature of the job. Possibly a study of these individuals may be of great importance in developing new kinds of selection criteria. One might expect that people who gain satisfaction from contextual factors would do well in jobs with a low potentiality for job-related satisfactions. The converse might also hold.

PART III · The Implications

These are our findings. The way in which our analysis proceeded during the past section demonstrates, we feel, the success of the approach we adopted. It may be recalled that we started out to study the factors-attitudes-effects unit as it was reported by single individuals. Obviously our analysis has not been restricted to an impressionistic account of these F-A-E units. There has been independent analysis of factors in the objective situation, of factors in the psychological reactions of the individual, and of effects. Yet during our discussion we were able to deal with the interrelationships among these factors and effects, to move back and forth among the components of the sequences of events as we discussed the nature of the data.

We must now address ourselves to the broader significance of the findings. Our stated purpose also included the search for a fresh point of view in the study of people's attitudes towards their jobs. Do the data we collected add up to anything? The next three sections consist of our answers to that question.

First, in Chapter 11, we should like to expand and restate one of the hypotheses with which we began. It turned out that the tentative suggestion in our analysis of the literature that satisfiers are different from dissatisfiers was abundantly confirmed. As a result of our study we can specify more clearly than was previously possible the nature of that difference. Chapter 12 explores some of the specific implications of this major finding. Finally, in Chapter 13 we try to present this "new look" at the bases of job attitudes within a broad framework derived from the thinking of students of society about the role of work. We end with our suggestions for implementation.

Chapter 11   A Hypothesis
                    Restated and Expanded

O ur study has been concerned with one of the most frequently
investigated areas of job attitudes. The central question is "What
do people want from their jobs?" In our previous survey of the
literature we uncovered a total of 155 studies, published between
the years 1920 and 1954, which purported to present data in
answer to this question. Figure 2 portrays the steady rise in
interest in this question. In the five-year period, 1920 to 1924,
a single study related to this question was found. In the five-year
period, 1950 to 1954, a total of sixty-seven such studies had been
published. Add to this large total the ever-increasing number of
opinion and exhortative writings in this area, and we must con-
clude that the answer to this question is conceived as the crucial
source to the successful motivation of the worker.

It has become almost axiomatic in the field of industrial relations that a knowledge of what a worker wants from his job is
essential to sound personnel practice. It is often equally axiomatic that sound personnel practice, because of practical considerations, must be based on factors other than those that sup-
posedly satisfy the worker's needs from his job. In a recent
article by Robert N. McMurry, published in the *Harvard Business
Review,* some of these practical considerations are described.
Among the obstacles that present-day industry puts in the way
of a wholly "humanistic or democratic plan of administration"
McMurry lists the need of superiors to keep the power in their
hands, the need for uniformity of practice, and the bureaucratic
traditions of most corporations (44).

Since this is such a wide open field for speculation and ex-

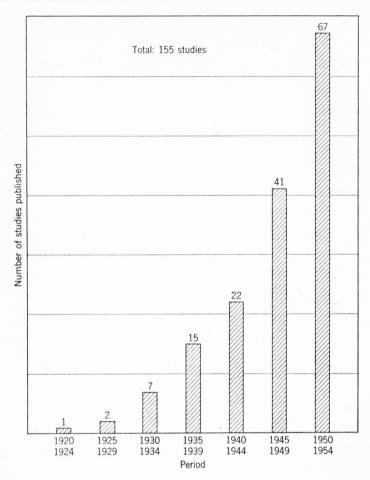

Figure 2. *Publication of evidence relating job factors and job attitudes.* From Herzberg, F., B. Mausner, R. Peterson, and D. Capwell. *Job Attitudes: Review of Research and Opinion*, Psychological Service, Pittsburgh, Pennsylvania, 1957.

pertise, any choice of personnel philosophy can be supported by the postulation of appropriate needs. Believers in a "modern" human relations approach to motivation and morale will find abundant support in studies which demonstrate that the basic need of the worker is to be treated with dignity and with an awareness of his unique personality. At the same time, those of the "hardheaded" school of industrial relations can find many sources from experience as well as from research studies to support their view that man works for the almighty dollar. For all the shades of gray between these two extreme positions both experiential and research evidence is available. It is disturbing to the social scientist to find that the accumulation of data from research provides evidence for all possible answers to the essential question of, "What do people want from their jobs?"

The first obvious explanation for this state of affairs is to point to the vast differences in the methods employed as well as in the excellence of research designs. Even slight changes in the phrasing of questions for eliciting job-attitude responses have repeatedly demonstrated major effects on the information obtained. Similarly, the nature of the populations studied will exert a strong effect on the results.

Many practitioners of personnel administration, however, accept the seemingly variable nature of the job needs expressed by employees as evidence for the irrationality of employee motivation. Since what the individual says he wants from his job is transient and unsystematic, a sound personnel practice will ignore what the individual says and tell him what he wants. This is often done through a company's communication media. Information is distributed about benefit programs, job security, safety, company leadership in the field, and the free-enterprise economic system. The ostensible purpose of these programs is to keep employees informed, but it is evident that an equal purpose is to bring to the attention of the employees the areas in which they should gain their satisfactions. The need to rely today on this subtle approach to teaching workers their proper job needs arises from the failure of the more open methods practiced under "paternalistic" management. It is interesting to note that studies of management-employee empathy, in which management has tried to predict the needs of the worker, have shown that management is unable to make valid predictions (28). In a more systematic and direct manner the unions have also attempted to "educate" the worker as to what his job needs are. Studies of union-worker empathy have shown an almost equal lack of success in union officials' predictions of workers' wants as has been true of management (49, 50). Nonetheless, wherever the union has been in competition with management in determining what the employee should feel he wants from his job, the union has been eminently more successful.

Other observers of employee motivation have felt that there is some order to the seeming capriciousness of employee wants. They adopt from a theory of motivation by Maslow the concept of a "need hierarchy" in which the various needs of an individual can be placed on a hierarchy of prepotency. According to this theory, "when a need is fairly well satisfied, the next prepotent (higher) need emerges, in turn to dominate the conscious life and to serve as the center of organization of behavior, since gratified needs are not active motivators" (40, 41).

In Maslow's system the hierarchy begins with the basic physiological needs as initially the most prepotent in the motivation of the organism and extends through a variety of psychological needs as initially less prepotent, but ready to become more prepotent when the physiological needs are satisfied. As this concept has been extended to the problems of job motivation, the basic biological motivations are generally found to be at a sufficient level of satisfaction so that the hierarchy lies within the various psychological and social needs of the individual. This concept has led many people to feel that the worker can never be satisfied with his job. How are you going to solve the dilemma of trying to motivate workers who have a continuously revolving set of needs? Since each individual may present at any one time a different scramble of his psychological need list, a systematic personnel practice hoping to cater to the most prepotent needs of its entire working force is defeated by the nature of the probabilities. Forgetting for a moment the individual "need hierarchies," it can be argued that there is sufficient homogeneity within various groups of employees to make for a relative similarity of "need hierarchies" within each group. Even so, the changes in prepotency for the group will occur, and personnel administration will have to keep up with them. For some who hold to this point of view personnel administration is reduced to the essential of labor-management bargaining. For others it means that personnel programs must be geared to be sensitive to the changes that are continually taking place in the needs of the employees. And since this can be done only by the supervisors, the training of supervisors in understanding human motivation, the factors underlying it, and the therapeutic or manipulative skills with which to cope with it is the most essential ingredient to any industrial-relations program.

We doubt that no general laws can be stated in the study of job attitudes.   Is the answer to the question, "What do people want from their jobs?" always to be, "It depends"?   We certainly need a less pessimistic approach if the rewards from better motivation for both industry and individuals are to be gained.   One systematic set of relationships did emerge both from our study of the literature and from the findings presented in Chapter 8 of this book.   It was noticed in the reviews of the literature that different results were achieved when the study design was concerned with what made people happy with their jobs as opposed to those studies directed toward discovering the factors that led to job dissatisfaction.   The factors in our study that made people happy with their jobs turned out to be different from the factors that made people unhappy with their jobs.   What does this finding imply for the general problem raised in the present section?

One of the basic habits of scientific thinking is to conceive of variables as operating on a continuum.   According to this, a factor that influences job attitudes should influence them in such a way that the positive or negative impact of the same factor should lead to a corresponding increase or decrease in morale. Perhaps some of the confusion as to what workers want from their jobs stems from the habit of thinking that factors influencing job attitudes operate along such a continuum.   But what if they don't?   What if there are some factors that affect job attitudes only in a positive direction?   If so, the presence of these factors would act to increase the individual's job satisfaction, but the failure of these factors to occur would not necessarily give rise to job dissatisfaction.   Theoretically, given an individual operating from a neutral point, with neither positive nor negative attitudes towards his job, the satisfaction of the factors, which we may call the "satisfiers," would increase his job satisfaction beyond the neutral point.   The absence of satisfaction to these factors would merely drop him back to this neutral level but would not turn him into a dissatisfied employee.   Contrariwise, there should be a group of factors that would act as "dissatisfiers."   Existence of these negative factors would lead to an unhappy employee.   The satisfying of these factors, however, would not create a happy employee.   This basic difference between "satisfiers" and "dissatisfiers," which operate in only one direction in determining the job attitudes of workers, was one of the hypotheses of our study.   In our own data, of course, we found that this unidirectional effect was truer of dissatisfiers than satisfiers.

There is still the possibility of a fluctuating "need hierarchy" operating within the group of satisfiers or dissatisfiers; or the order of importance of the components of these groups may be reasonably uniform for groups of workers who share certain common psychological characteristics. As we have seen, the data of our study do not permit us to draw any hard and fast conclusions on this point. Future research may be able to pinpoint the order of importance of the various satisfiers or dissatisfiers. Even better, we may be able to relate any given order of importance either to the situation or to the kind of people with whom we are dealing.

Be that as it may, our study has enabled us to lay down some lines of stability in the analysis of job attitudes. We are, therefore, a step beyond the fatalistic assumption that no secure conclusions can be drawn from a study of the needs people fulfill in their jobs. In the next section we examine at some length the implications for industry of the specific elements of lawfulness we have been able to introduce into this field.

Chapter 12   Motivation
                                  versus Hygiene

L et us summarize briefly our answer to the question, "What do people want from their jobs?" When our respondents reported feeling happy with their jobs, they most frequently described factors related to their tasks, to events that indicated to them that they were successful in the performance of their work, and to the possibility of professional growth. Conversely, when feelings of unhappiness were reported, they were not associated with the job itself but with conditions that *surround* the doing of the job. These events suggest to the individual that the context in which he performs his work is unfair or disorganized and as such represents to him an unhealthy psychological work environment. Factors involved in these situations we call factors of *hygiene*, for they act in a manner analogous to the principles of medical hygiene. Hygiene operates to remove health hazards from the environment of man. It is not a curative; it is, rather, a preventive. Modern garbage disposal, water purification, and air-pollution control do not cure diseases, but without them we should have many more diseases. Similarly, when there are deleterious factors in the context of the job, they serve to bring about poor job attitudes. Improvement in these factors of hygiene will serve to remove the impediments to positive job attitudes. Among the factors of hygiene we have included supervision, interpersonal relations, physical working conditions, salary, company policies and administrative practices, benefits, and job security. When these factors deteriorate to a level below that which the employee considers acceptable, then job dissatisfaction ensues. However, the reverse does not hold true. When the job context can be characterized as optimal, we will not get dissatisfaction, but neither will we get much in the way of positive attitudes.

The factors that lead to positive job attitudes do so because they satisfy the individual's need for self-actualization in his work. The concept of self-actualization, or self-realization, as a man's ultimate goal has been focal to the thought of many personality theorists. For such men as Jung, Adler, Sullivan, Rogers, and Goldstein the supreme goal of man is to fulfill himself as a creative, unique individual according to his own innate potentialities and within the limits of reality. When he is deflected from this goal he becomes, as Jung says, "a crippled animal."

Man tends to actualize himself in every area of his life, and his job is one of the most important areas. The conditions that surround the doing of the job cannot give him this basic satisfaction; they do not have this potentiality. It is only from the performance of a task that the individual can get the rewards that will reinforce his aspirations. It is clear that although the factors relating to the doing of the job and the factors defining the job context serve as goals for the employee, the nature of the motivating qualities of the two kinds of factors are essentially different. Factors in the job context meet the needs of the individual for avoiding unpleasant situations. In contrast to this motivation by meeting avoidance needs, the job factors reward the needs of the individual to reach his aspirations. These effects on the individual can be conceptualized as actuating approach rather than avoidance behavior. Since it is in the approach sense that the term motivation is most commonly used, we designate the job factors as the "motivators," as opposed to the extra-job factors, which we have labeled the factors of hygiene. It should be understood that both kinds of factors meet the needs of the employee; but it is primarily the "motivators" that serve to bring about the kind of job satisfaction and, as we saw in the section dealing with the effects of job attitudes, the kind of improvement in performance that industry is seeking from its work force.

We can now say something systematic about what people want from their jobs. For the kind of population that we sampled, and probably for many other populations as well, the wants of employees divide into two groups. One group revolves around the need to develop in one's occupation as a source of personal growth. The second group operates as an essential base to the first and is associated with fair treatment in compensation, supervision, working conditions, and administrative practices. The fulfillment of the needs of the second group does not motivate the individual to high levels of job satisfaction and, as shown in Chapter 9, to extra performance on the job. All we can expect from satisfying the needs for hygiene is the prevention of dissatisfaction and poor job performance.

In the light of this distinction, we can account for much of the lack of success that industry has had in its attempts to motivate employees. Let us examine two of the more ubiquitous avenues through which industry has hoped to gain highly motivated employees: human-relations training for supervisors and wage-incentive systems.

As part of this era of human relations, supervisory training directed toward improving the interpersonal relationships between superior and subordinate has been widely incorporated into industrial-relations programs. These programs have been initiated with expectations of bringing about positive job attitudes and, hopefully, increased performance on the job. When we examine the results of our study, we find interpersonal relationships appearing in an exceedingly small number of the high sequences; in only 15 per cent of the low sequences are poor interpersonal relationships with the superior reported. The negligible role which interpersonal relationships play in our data tallies poorly with the assumption basic to most human-relations training programs that the way in which a supervisor gets along with his people is the single most important determinant of morale. Supervisory training in human relations is probably essential to the maintenance of good hygiene at work. This is particularly true for the many jobs, both at rank-and-file and managerial levels, in which modern industry offers little chance for the operation of the motivators. These jobs are atomized, cut and dried, monotonous. They offer little chance for responsibility and achievement and thus little opportunity for self-actualization. It is here that hygiene is exceptionally important. The fewer the opportunities for the "motivators" to appear, the greater must be the hygiene offered in order to make the work tolerable. A man who finds his job challenging, exciting, and satisfying will perhaps tolerate a difficult supervisor. But to expect such programs to pay dividends beyond the effects that hygiene provides is going contrary to the nature of job motivation. In terms of the approach-avoidance concept, the advocates of human relations have suggested that by rewarding the avoidance needs of the individual you will achieve the desired approach behavior. But a more creative design will not emerge from an engineer as a result of fair supervisory treatment. To achieve the more creative design, one or more of the motivators must be present, a task that is interesting to the engineer, a task in which he can exercise responsibility and independence, a task that allows for some concrete achievement. The motivators fit the need for creativity, the hygiene factors satisfy the need for fair treatment, and it is thus that the appropriate incentive must be present to achieve the desired job attitude and job performance.

The failure to get positive returns in both job attitudes and job performance from rewarding the avoidance needs of the individual is most clearly seen in the use of monetary incentives. We have listed salary among the factors of hygiene, and as such it meets two kinds of avoidance needs of the employee. First is the avoidance of the economic deprivation that is felt when actual income is insufficient. Second, and generally of more significance in the times and for the kind of people covered by our study, is the need to avoid feelings of being treated unfairly. Salary and wages are very frequently at the top of the list of factors describing answers to the question, "What don't you like about your job?" in morale surveys. They are at the middle of the list of answers to the question, "What do you want from your job?" We have explained this difference in emphasis by our distinction between factors that lead to job satisfaction and the factors that contribute to job dissatisfaction. Asking people what is important to them in their jobs will bring responses that we have classified as "motivators." The atmosphere of the usual morale survey encourages people to emphasize sources of dissatisfaction.

Where morale surveys have differentiated between dissatisfaction with amount of salary as opposed to the equity of salary, the latter looms as the more important source of dissatisfaction. In two consecutive morale surveys by the senior author, in which the employees were requested to illustrate their dissatisfaction or satisfaction with the various items on the morale questionnaire with critical incidents, the comments on the equity of salary greatly outnumbered the comments on the absolute amount of salary. All 1382 employees surveyed were at the supervisory level (21).

How then can we explain the success of the many employee motivational schemes that seem to rely directly on the use of wage incentives and bonuses? Reports on the Lincoln Electric Company of Cleveland, Ohio (37), and the George A. Hormel meat-packing plant at Austin, Minnesota (7), suggest good examples of the efficacy of money incentives for increasing production, job satisfaction, and company loyalty. But let us examine for a moment the nature of these programs and the nature of their success in the light of the findings presented here.

First, there are many other ingredients to these plans which are generally given less attention than they merit, ingredients that combine a large proportion of the factors that we have found to be motivators. The formation of Lincoln's Advisory Board and Hormel's Business Improvement Committee both resulted from attempts to increase job content and job responsibility by giving workers knowledge of, and responsibility for, operations and improvements. *Both operate on the theory that the "boss" cannot know everything about all the work processes, that the workers are experts in their fields, and that their knowledge is of great value.* Lincoln Electric, which is not unionized, has the additional advantage of being able to advance workers on the basis of merit, not seniority. James E. Lincoln, president of the company, says that "money is of relatively small importance. Beyond enough for our real needs, money itself is valued less for what it will buy than as an evidence of successful skill in achievement (37)." Money thus earned as a direct reward for outstanding individual performance is a reinforcement of the motivators of *recognition* and *achievement*. It is not hygiene as is the money given in across-the-board wage increases.

The Scanlon plan is a system for involving employees of a company in the improvement of production by the distribution of savings in labor costs to all of the personnel of a participating company. This aspect of participation and of increased responsibility is the real secret of whatever success the Scanlon plan and its imitators have achieved. Lincoln Electric is implementing man's natural striving for self-realization. No man wants to be just a cog in a wheel. Lincoln says, "The most insistent incentive is the development of self-respect and the respect of

others. Earnings that are the reward for outstanding performance, progress, and responsibility are signs that he is a man
among men. The worker must feel that he is part of a worth-
while project and that the project succeeded because his ability
was needed in it. Money alone will not do the job."

When incentive systems do not permit any of the motivators
to operate, then any increase in performance or in apparent job
satisfaction is misleading. For in these instances the removal
of a decrement in performance by the elimination of job dissatisfaction is often mistakenly referred to as a positive gain in
performance. That voluntary restriction of output is practiced
on an enormous scale is common knowledge in industry (26, 27,
58). The existence of a standard of "a fair day's work" has been
well documented in systematic studies by industrial psychologists
and sociologists as well as industrial engineers. It is likely that
poor hygiene will depress performance below the level of "the
fair day's work." Correction of this poor hygiene, or the application of monetary incentives not related to motivators, may return performance to the norm. The improvement produced
under these circumstances is actually far less than one could
obtain were motivators to be introduced.

Are good job attitudes and company loyalty engendered by
these incentive plans? The surface answer often seems to be
yes. Employees in such companies will report that they like
working for their companies, but the "liking" seems to be little
more than the absence of disliking, their satisfaction little more
than the absence of dissatisfaction. Blum reports on the Hormel
packinghouse workers in this regard:

> If I had to summarize workers' feelings about the company in
> one sentence, I would repeat the words of a worker: "If a man is
> going to work for anybody else, it's hard to beat Hormel." It is
> the single most often heard expression in any conversation about
> the company. I have never heard a worker express an uncondi-
> tional acceptance of the company as an organization to work
> for (7).

Are they really saying they like their work? Or are they
merely saying that they have found a place to work in which
life is not unbearable?

What is the evidence? According to Blum's report, shop talk
is deafening by its absence when the work day is over. There
seems to be a deliberate effort on the part of the employees to

repress any mention of their jobs away from the plant. Contrast this with the unceasing shop talk reported by Walker in his study of steel workers at the National Tube Company of Ellwood City, Pennsylvania (56). His description of their jobs emphasizes the large number of motivators present. They are not running away from their work at the shift bell. They continue to live their jobs at home. The employees of Hormel seem to be psychologically running away from their jobs. Their extra effort, while it increases production, albeit probably not to the level of which they are capable, is not indicative of positive job attitudes. Rather it provides the means for escape from a job toward which their attitudes are little better than neutral. The sooner they finish the job, the sooner they can get away from it; the more money they can earn, the more effective their escape in pleasant living off the job. It is doubtful that the true production potential of these workers is being tapped; it is undeniable that the incentive system, along with other hygienic factors, serves to make their jobs tolerable.

The definition of *hygiene* and *motivation* and the relationship of these complexes of factors to the behavior of men at work has many implications for industrial practice. In the next section we try to explore these implications after setting the findings of our study in an historical background.

Chapter 13   Perspective

This is the point at which to evaluate the implications of our findings. Two questions have to be answered. First, are the findings we have derived from a study of 200 middle-management men generally applicable beyond this limited sample? Second, what are the implications of these findings for industry in particular and for the community-at-large in general? Clearly, the importance of the answer to the second question hinges on the answer to the first. If the findings of this study are consonant with our general knowledge of men at work, then the implications derived from these findings will be of great moment.*

A number of steps are traversed in answering these questions. The determination of the universality of the findings of this study begins with an analysis of the relationship to his work of primitive man and continue with a brief survey of the history of men at work. Next, a wide range of data from studies of contemporary life are examined in order to create a frame of reference against which the findings of the present study can

* Since the writing of this book, there has appeared a brilliant discussion of the nature of work by Hannah Arendt (2). In this Dr. Arendt distinguishes on a linguistic basis between "labor" and "work." Apparently almost all Indo-European languages have two terms for productive human activity. *Oeuvre* and *travail*, *werk* and *arbeit* are examples. Labor is related to the cyclical and biological nature of man; it produces objects which are essential to life but are immediately consumed. It is related to reproduction (the term is the same) and thus inferentially to pain. Work is a function of man the fabricator. Its products are lasting and are a source of satisfaction *in themselves*, not only because they fulfill biological needs. Labor is private activity; it leads to no increase in renown for the individual. Work is public, and its fruits are productive of history and of individual reputation.

It is apparent that in our book we have been speaking primarily of work, as Arendt defines it, rather than of labor. It is likely, therefore, that the entire discussion in this last chapter is meaningful only when work is involved and that the motives we speak of for work cannot, in the nature of things, be made available for labor.

120

be interpreted.   Last, we follow these trains of thought and develop recommendations for industry in particular and for society
in general.

The Meaning of Work in a Primitive Society

Much romantic nonsense has been written about primitive
man.   A number of social critics have contrasted his presumed
close contact with nature, his high level of craftsmanship, and
the integration of his work into the aesthetic, religious, and
social activities of his group with the mad and purposeless frenzy
of civilized man, chasing ill-defined goals with a ceaseless round
of meaningless activity.   Anyone familiar with the first-hand
reports of anthropologists would recognize the false emphasis
in this picture.   Life in primitive societies is hard and filled with
backbreaking toil.   There is relatively little opportunity for individual growth and development because of the necessity for
constant emphasis on sheer subsistence.   In a society which
spends 70 to 80 per cent of its labor on the mere growing of
food there is relatively little left over for the fullest development
of the individual.

We have no actual data on the attitudes of primitive man towards his work.   Ethnographers have rarely asked the proper
questions.   However, the findings of our study have some implications for an understanding of primitive man, and it may be
that the universality of our findings would be demonstrated by
work with primitive communities.   The labor of primitive man
fits very well the description given by the factors found in our
"short-range high" sequences of events.   That is, primitive man
spends most of his energies in activities whose goals are directly
related to his immediate needs.   The fulfillment of these goals
can be derived through these activities.   Primitive man does
work at producing the food he consumes, the clothing he wears,
the dwelling in which he lives.   Thus one could postulate that
the work of primitive man fulfills, to some extent at least, the
needs for "motivation" in work that have been reported by our
sample.   It is probably also true that the close relationship between work and aesthetics, religion, and social relations, which
has been described innumerable times by anthropologists, increases the motivation for work.   There is no doubt, for example,

that the builder of a primitive canoe, who is fulfilling aesthetic as well as economic needs, probably shows a high level of motivation in our sense. Similarly, the carver of a totem pole, who is fulfilling religious and social needs, probably has an equally high level of motivation. Primitive man does not separate basic economic from aesthetic and religious needs. The totem pole, as insurance for the salmon run, is as closely related to subsistence as soil testing is to a scientific farmer.

The important difference between primitive man and modern man at his best is in the time scale of activities and in the potentiality for individual growth. In primitive societies there is relatively little opportunity for the individual to break the mold of tradition and to develop his unique modes of behavior. Undoubtedly some primitives do grow in individual responsibility and skills in their craftsmanship. However, this is probably rather rare in comparison to similar opportunities available to certain strata of our own society.

Thus we can postulate that the primitive man should show a high level of positive attitudes toward his work because of the fact that this work is directly related to the fulfillment of his immediate needs. As civilization develops, man gives up this direct relationship between work and biological needs and substitutes the indirect relationships that develop in a society in which division of labor and a money economy obtain. That this change represents a serious loss for a great many individuals in advanced societies has been pointed out by social critics.

Transition to the Machine Age

In primitive societies the major source of energy is the contraction of muscles, human or animal. As these societies coalesced into the great classical civilizations, the sources of energy remained the same; the role of the individual changed greatly. With a growing division of labor and a diversification of tasks, the mass of human beings became subjugated to a system in which their work was now no longer directly related to the fulfillment of their individual needs. Again, although we have no direct evidence, it is probable that most people who lived in classical days in Egypt, Greece, China, or Rome found relatively little satisfaction in their activities, since their duties were not only physically wearing but also required almost nothing in the way of skill or diversity. More than this, their work was lacking in most of the other characteristics of motivation, as these were derived from our study. The slave, who receives his subsistence from his master, cannot obtain any sense of achievement or growth from a meaningless round of activities.

A sizable minority *did* retain their primitive skills and developed into a new group of craftsmen. For these individuals, although work was now no longer related to the fulfillment of biological needs, it did lead to the fulfillment of a new set of needs still flowing directly from the activities of work itself. The records and observations that we have of the lives of craftsmen would lead us to assume that the end product of their craftsmanship was of value in itself. Although we have no direct evidence of this, it is a fairly good inference that the psychological income to be derived from the weaving of cloth, the sculpturing of stone, or the making of fine chased armor in medieval times was very great.

As the use of human and animal muscle as a major source of power gave way to the machine, the man who had once been a common laborer or a craftsman now became a machine tender. Although the machine liberated much of humanity from the necessity for direct physical toil, it condemned its new slaves to an entirely different kind of bondage. The essence of machine operation is repetitiveness and uniformity. The tender of the machine may work very hard, but he has relatively little control over the outcome of his work.

He has even less control than did the handworker of classical and feudal times. Thus, if any of the satisfactions of craftsmanship were available to workers in the pre-Machine Age, they were lost as the Machine Age developed.

We do not mean to infer that motivation vanished completely with the coming of the Machine Age. There were still many individual craftsmen. In addition, new classes of individuals arose whose work was related to the planning, supervision, and exploitation of the work of machines and their tenders. The transition from the pre-Industrial to the Industrial Era therefore provided enormous opportunities for motivation to a small minority, at least, of the human race. For the rest of mankind the motives to work were clearly of the kind that we have labeled "hygienic." The end product of work, not related to the activities themselves, was minimal subsistence at best and a level of living well below this at worst.

Work in the Contemporary World

The present century has seen some important changes in the pattern described for the preceding two centuries. The desperate urgency that pressed the mass of working people during the past is very much less powerful. In the Western world the satisfaction of subsistence needs is at a higher level than has ever before been reached by the human race. Here, productivity is high; poverty is relatively rare. The dictates of Poor Richard have lost much of their force. Meanwhile, the growing complexity of social organization and the disparity between an official ideology, which stressed frontier virtues, and the actualities of civilized life have led to innumerable social ailments.

What are these social ills as they have been described by critics of contemporary society? First and foremost, as the social critics see it, is an alienation between the individual and the groups of which he is a member. This can be traced to many causes. One of these causes is the very discrepancy just mentioned between official ideology and actualities. We are indebted to Émile Durkheim (15) for an elegant formulation of this conflict. He uses the term "anomie" (a lack of norms or guideposts) for the condition of the individual who has high ideals and a lively sense of ethics but who is forced to compromise these ethics and ideals in everyday life. When such an alienation between values and the realities of the world takes place, the result is a feeling of rootlessness and distance between people.

The loss of strength in the bonds holding individuals together may have other sources than the anomie described by Durkheim. Typical analyses of these other sources come from a psychoanalyst such as Erich Fromm (17) or a political scientist such as Sebastian DeGrazia (13). As they describe the contemporary scene, the sheer size and complexity of our urban civilization may itself contribute to this sense of distance among people. Aside from this, however, one of the greatest villains in reducing the meaningfulness of the relationship between people is a change in the way in which social activity is coordinated and directed. In less complex societies the coordination and direction of social activity was based directly on the face-to-face relationships of individuals. The guild workshop and the feudal barony were run by authority inherent in the master workman and the baron. The master workman's authority came from his skills; the baron's authority from his lineage. In our more complex world the personal rule of the chief is supplanted by the rule of bureaucratic law. Under this dispensation individuals wield authority not because of their skill or personal quality but because of the offices they occupy. As a result, the exercise of authority is rarely based on the use of personal judgment. If one's authority comes from law, then the carrying out of this authority is rigorously bound by predetermined rules set by the bureaucracy. Development of close ties between master and follower is difficult; at best it is tangential to the actual direction of work.

The Consequences of Bureaucracy

Does this change have consequences beyond the weakening of personal ties? It may. We have noted earlier that the profoundest motivation to work comes from the recognition of individual achievement and from the sense of personal growth in responsibility. It is likely that neither of these can flourish too well in a bureaucratic situation. For the supervisor the opportunity to exercise personal judgment is negligible. He works within the framework of the system of rules, and since his authority comes from his position rather than from any personal characteristics he may have he is likely to stray very rarely from the narrow paths determined by these rules. There can be little sense of achievement, little perception of growth in the exercise of an authority bound by the "book."

For the subordinate, and in a bureaucracy everyone is a subordinate, the situation is as bad. Again the rules, as interpreted by the supervisor as well as by the book, determine not only what is to be done but *how* it is to be done. The exercise of ingenuity and initiative is discouraged. For one thing, it is too disconcerting to everyone to have individuals depart from the usual procedure; for another, there are few rewards offered for such departures.

Since both supervisors and workers are rigorously bound by the predetermined rules, it is likely that extraneous considerations remote from the actual carrying out of tasks come to play an increasing role in the attempts of supervisors to motivate their workers. If you cannot give workers leeway in the way they do their work, and if most people measure up uniformly to the demands of the organization, the basis for reward cannot have anything much to do with actual success or failure in the job. Since this is true at almost every level of organized authority, one might predict a decrease in the available amount of motivation as the rigidity and complexity of bureaucracy increase. We shall discuss the further implications of this development shortly.

The Search for Motivation

In the nineteenth century the theory of the economic man was basic to all notions of motivation for work. The economic man as master buys and sells in the cheapest market. The economic man as worker sells his labor at the best price he can get for it. With changes in the structure of society and with the growing sophistication derived from the new sciences of man, this nineteenth-century view became untenable. Of course, the manipulation of economic incentives is still far from obsolete. The economic incentive is still hopefully applied to the hourly worker in a bonus or to the vice-president in an offer of a stock option.

And yet, as the present century has progressed, there has been a more and more frantic search for ways of motivating people in industry beyond the exercise of economic power. This is the goal of innumerable courses in human relations, in which supervisors are urged to learn their subordinates' first names, to smile at them, to treat them "as if they were human beings." * The gospel of human relations has been accompanied by an increase in "fringe" benefits. The very term expresses the characteristics of these rewards as tangential to the work for which they are a partial reward. Of course, these benefits have been given not only in a desire to improve human relations but also in response to the demands of trade unions at the lower levels of employment and of the market for executives at the higher levels. Thus the

---

* We do not intend to cast aspersions on the large number of carefully worked out training programs in human relations carried out by qualified professionals. These courses, in their attempt to attack specific evils, often do a great deal to eliminate bad hygiene.

great corporation, with its company newspapers and athletic teams, its feeding facilities, and its lush working surroundings, is saying in effect, "we will treat you well, and we hope you will work faithfully for us."

The "conventional wisdom" of personnel relations is full of arguments to the effect that workers who are alienated from their jobs and their employers work poorly. They leave their jobs readily, they absent themselves easily, and are prone to mental illness and maladjustment. In an inductive leap for which the objective evidence is very slim the hope is often expressed that the improvement in these fringe conditions will not only lead to a lessening of the ill-consequences of poor morale but also to the direct, positive stimulation of the worker to improved work.

One of the most important sources for this presumption is the series of studies carried on at the Hawthorne plants of the Western Electric Company by Elton Mayo and his colleagues from the Harvard Business School (42, 51). As we saw in our survey of sources in Chapter 1, these studies stressed the positive effects on worker output of the personal interest shown by supervisors. The end result of these studies was the institution of a counseling program to which workers could come in and attempt to solve their personal problems (14). Another facet of the Hawthorne studies, in which the existence of certain social groups among workers was identified, led to an increasing interest on the part of industry in the social characteristics of work groups.

In Chapter 1 we mentioned the work of Lewin and his successors, which led to the development of the notion of participation as well as the parallel development of "employee-centered supervision." The end result of this activity was a focus on the individual worker as a human being, with needs and motives infinitely more complex than the economic drives that had been the sole resource of earlier thinking. Many specific investigations, too numerous to cite here, proved the point that workers *liked* to have a voice in the decisions that affected them and that they responded with positive emotions when they were treated as individual human beings rather than as an undifferentiated mass.

The idea, first, that the participation of subordinates in decision making was possible, and, second, that it was desirable has been the subject of a great deal of controversy. To some it has been the core of a movement toward industrial democracy that almost has the force of a new religion. To others it has the odor of quackery (59). There is no question that a genuine attempt to extend the scope of participation has been made in some places. The interpretation of these attempts and of their purported success is far from clear. Our own discussion of the potency of monetary incentives has appealed to the notion of participation as an explanation of the success of such devices as the Scanlon plan (see Chapter 12).

Actually, participation cannot be viewed as a nostrum, the application of which will cure all ills and restore a pristine fervor for work. The close of this section includes some final comments about our own views of the kind of participation that would be most useful and most practicable in the contemporary industrial world.

In the last hundred years there has been a growing realization of a sickness in our society and that one source of this sickness is the relationship of people to their work. The fact that so many are now looking to leisure activities to absorb the bulk of their energies is certainly an indication. The cures for this illness have been sought in attempts on the part of industry to increase the warmth of interpersonal relationships by human-relations training, in attempts to improve the context in which work is carried on by an increase in fringe benefits and in the pleasantness of working conditions, and by an artificial attempt to inject a certain amount of participation into the otherwise routinized lives of most people in industry by a stress on group processes and group discussion.

The Managerial and Professional World

Let us look a little more closely at the world of managerial and professional people, since they, after all, make up the group sampled in the present study. Managerial and professional jobs, it is commonly reported, have been diluted seriously in recent times. In a parody of the assembly line managerial and professional workers are assigned small pieces of work seen as a whole by a favored few. This rationalization of the work process has, in places, been carried to such an extreme that individuals are rarely responsible for carrying through a complete task.

This dilution is often accompanied by an increase in stress on group activities. The research on the existence of social groupings among lower level workers and the discovery that these groupings are highly functional on those levels has helped the trend to an insistence on group activity in many areas in which it is far from appropriate.

When the relationship between an individual and his accomplishments is hard to discern because of the rationalization of jobs and the stress on group work, it is almost inevitable that the quality of interpersonal relationships becomes a highly important criterion for the evaluation of individuals. As William H. Whyte, Jr., in *The Organization Man* (59), Vance Packard in *The Hidden Persuaders* (47), and others have pointed out with alarm, American industry is relying more and more on measures of personality and temperament as a primary source for the evaluation of new entrants into the ranks of management. Several recent studies have noted that executives are more often than not fired for failure in qualities remotely related to actual job performance. One paper presents data of considerable value in indicating the relative influence of "knowledge lacks" and "personality lacks" in executive failures (43). Personality lacks are far more often the reason for termination of employment than knowledge lacks. McFarland, the author, states that "more than nine out of ten such people (managerial and professional workers) lost their positions for reasons that do not even remotely pertain to know-how. These people got fired because they had poor health, poor personalities, and poor dispositions; because they talked too much, were careless, untidy, intemperate, and unreliable.

It is inevitable that people living in such a world should learn to respond properly in terms of the system of rewards and punishments offered to them. A study made by the senior author in several companies whose managerial employees were appraised by psychological tests and interviews shows no relationship between intelligence and aptitude and the success of managerial individuals as defined by their ranks or by their salaries.

The usual moral of this story is that industry must search even more unceasingly for the proper attributes of personality in its potential managers and professionals. In a situation in which initial hiring and later advancement depend not on skill but on personality individuals learn to avoid too great a display of tech-

TABLE 17

Correlations between Abilities and Salary

	Logical Reasoning	Verbal Reasoning	Critical Thinking
Steel company (N = 58)	0.10	0.10	0.18
Electronics company (N = 61)	0.23	0.10	0.18

1. Correlations reported are with the effect of age removed.
2. Salary is highly related to hierarchical positions.

nical skill. When the rewards of work are connected with behaviors not related to the actual tasks of the job, it is hardly surprising that the worker, whether foreman or company vice-president, soon learns a set of values revolving around these extraneous rewards. What we in this study have called hygiene becomes an end for much of existence.

The miracle is that in spite of all this the 200 people in our sample were able to speak of the moving and exciting moments in their lives in which they *did* have a genuine opportunity for achievement through the actual work of their jobs. Apparently, the feeling of growth in stature and responsibility is still the most exciting thing that can happen to someone in our society.

The Consequences for the Individual and for Society

An individual living in such a world is debarred from seeking real satisfactions in his work. Interpersonal relationships outside work are overloaded; the hobby often becomes a substitute for the job. But the hobby cannot give the complete sense of growth, the sense of striving towards a meaningful goal, that can be found in one's life work. A carpenter's workshop in the basement and a neatly groomed backyard are no substitutes for the direct relationship between work and the fulfillment of the individual's needs that we described for primitive man.

One wonders whether the sense of anomie, of the rootlessness and alienation which anthropologists, political scientists, and psychiatrists have found so serious in our world, is not at least in part a consequence of this overloading of interpersonal relationships due to the loss of the direct meaning of work.

What does this mean for society? It poses a real danger of an inflexible and uncreative society that will be unable to react adequately to the stresses posed by an always demanding world. If the major rewards in our society are hygienic, if conditions not related to the actual conduct of work are the major sources of satisfaction, there is little motivation for the fulfillment of the highest potentiality in the work of each individual. When such a society has to cease living off the fat of earlier creativity, it may very well suffer the fate undergone by earlier societies now no longer in existence. The world is full of the dusty ruins of empires that were not resilient enough to cope with barbarian invaders.

Suggestions

It would be foolhardy on our part to present a detailed recipe, on the basis of our study, for the cure of all the world's ills. However, the picture we have just drawn in conjunction with the evidence from our study points to certain conclusions, which to the writers, at least, are inescapable.

What concretely can we tell not only industry but all individuals concerned with the shaping of work? In general, the implications of our study can be summed up as an emphasis on a positive rather than a negative approach towards the morale of individuals. Our society has accepted, in the main, the negative approach to morale. Only the most antediluvian managers are resistant to the need to mitigate bad hygienic conditions in order to avoid turnover, absenteeism, and individual malfunction. We would certainly not urge a diminution in such programs. Our findings definitely support the notion that good hygiene will prevent many of the negative results of low morale.

Yet good hygiene cannot be an end in itself; it is merely a beginning. As we have pointed out, an overemphasis on hygiene carries within itself the seeds of trouble. It can lead to a greater and greater focus on the extraneous rewards that reside in the context of jobs. Our emphasis should be on the strengthening of motivators. The slogan could almost be raised, "Hygiene is not enough."

A number of areas in which motivation to work can be strengthened by an emphasis on the greater fulfillment of goals is directly related to the doing of work. As we discuss each of these areas, it will be clear that we cannot present precise and detailed accounts of how this can be done. Only the goals can be specified from the results of our study. The precise way in which increased motivation can be developed must await further research.

The Structure of Jobs

First, jobs must be restructured to increase to the maximum the ability of workers to achieve goals meaningfully related to the doing of the job. A number of issues is raised by this simple statement. It is apparent that the great bulk of production workers, except for craftsmen, is debarred from such rewards by the very nature of their jobs. Why? It is tempting to speculate on the psychological characteristics of jobs in which it is possible to get rewards directly related to the doing of the work. A look at the kinds of reports given by our respondents leads to one tentative conclusion. This is that the individual should have some measure of control over the way in which the job is done in order to realize a sense of achievement and of personal growth. Clearly, most assembly-line workers cannot have such control.

A new development in industry, however, will change this picture for a sizable proportion of workers. One fairly large segment of our economy is being automated. What effect has automation on this problem? Walker, in his recent study (57), has investigated intensively the effect of automation on people's attitudes towards their jobs. He finds that morale goes down when partial automation increases the need for rigid and routine work. In the final fully automated plant, however, an interesting phenomenon takes place. At first, the workers are bewildered and unhappy about the shift to jobs in which they are no longer physically active but in which they are perpetually tense, perpetually under the need to watch, think, and discriminate. How-

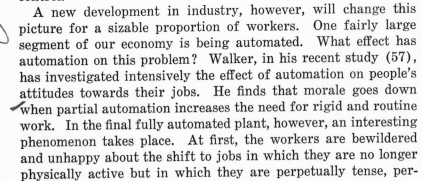

ever, an adjustment does take place, and then the ability of these workers to feel control over the over-all process of the plant leads to higher morale than ever. Automation carried out to its fullest may very well provide an environment in which the production worker, at least, can achieve some of the motivators about which we were speaking.

But automation affects professional and managerial personnel relatively little. In fact, the degree to which professional and managerial workers will increase in number as a result of automation makes the problems of this group more rather than less pressing. The frame of reference that automates factories will produce temptations to go further in the direction of stereotypy and regimentation at the professional and managerial level. Thus at the managerial level automation poses more dangers than it provides opportunities; nevertheless, wherever automation takes place the opportunity is given to management to show imagination and skill in the structuring of jobs so that the largest number of individuals can be given the highest level of motivation.

Should Jobs Be Made More Interesting?

The answer to this question is not simple. A movement has been in existence for some time that would increase the interest of jobs by broadening them. Is this what is being discussed here? It is not in the sense in which job broadening is usually viewed. If job broadening means a "Cook's tour" in which individuals have snippets of different activities, unrelated in any meaningful sense, then the mere addition of new activities should not be expected to increase motivation in the terms described in this book. Rotation from one activity to another would be successful only if the individual being rotated were able to integrate his various activities into achievements that have psychological meaning for him.

Furthermore, our data indicate that achievements in themselves are only a partial reward. The accumulation of achievement must lead to a feeling of personal growth in the individual, accompanied by a sense of increasing responsibility. Is interest in the operations of work a critical factor? Very likely, as we can see in our findings, interesting work is often the cue to a higher level of motivation. But it is difficult to predict in advance for any one individual what will or will not be interesting. Thus, the redesigning of jobs cannot be predicated upon an attempt to make them interesting. It is true, as it has always been, that the personnel worker will continue to attempt to fit each individual to the work which that individual finds most intrinsically rewarding. But that is not the point we are making here. Our point is that the jobs themselves have to be set up in such a way that, interest or no, the individual who carries them out can find that their operations lead to increased motivation.

The Problem of Selection

If one structures the jobs properly, one must also structure the selection process properly. There has been a good deal of reaction against the more naïve aspects of the exploitation of personality tests in selection. Yet our recommendation goes deeper than the protests of William H. Whyte against the manifest "unfairness" of the personality test or the analysis of application blanks for hidden characteristics. We wish to shift the emphasis from personality to the attempt to match an individual's work capacity with work he will be needed to do. This demands a continued close analysis of the actual kinds of abilities needed for each job and an equally close analysis of the potential abilities of applicants for work. Of course, there should be some recognition of the fact that in many jobs at high levels there are numerous combinations of abilities and temperaments that will lead to success in the same job for different reasons.

Supervision

What role did the supervisor play in the lives of the people in our sample? He was often made the villain in stories about times when morale was low. He almost never appeared as a *focus* for high morale. We may remember, however, that the supervisor did appear in a single, restricted role in stories about highs. He was frequently the source for the recognition of successful work.

There is another and more subtle aspect of supervision that

must be recognized. Even though this was not reported by our respondents, it is likely that a successful supervisor was often instrumental in structuring the work so that his subordinates *could* realize their ability for creative achievement. In the interdependent world of industry few people can fulfill their potentialities entirely by their own efforts. It is this latter aspect of the supervisor's task that we would like to stress in our recommendations.

Let us deal first with the supervisor's role as the dispenser of recognition. Typically, the formal vehicle for recognition is a merit rating of some kind. On this the individual depends for salary increases, promotions, and quality of assignments. It is brash of us to urge that merit ratings be tied as closely as possible to reliable and valid measures of actual performance. Psychologists, industrial engineers, and experts in management have been struggling for years with the problems of such ratings. That they have been relatively unsuccessful, that merit ratings are *not* a very dependable measure, is notorious. All we can do is point to the urgent necessity for further progress.

One development in the design of merit ratings has tended to diminish the possibility of progress. A heavy weight is often placed on personality factors. This beclouds the clarity of the rating as a reward for good work or punishment of bad.

In assessing the importance of recognition as a factor in positive job attitudes we have noted that it has little force in promoting long-range feelings of high morale, except when it is a part of the greater complex of motivational factors. This argues that the most important job of the supervisor is his organizational and planning function. The training of the upper level of supervisors in graduate schools of business or of industrial administration certainly focuses on problems of organization and planning. One wonders whether the preoccupation of human-relations training for the lower levels of supervision has not tended to dilute the more technical aspects of work at these levels. Beyond this, as we have previously suggested, it may be that the very structure of middle-management jobs has limited unduly the potential for organization and planning.

Our conclusion is that the single most important goal in the progress of supervision is the development of new insights into the role of the supervisor so that he may effectively plan and organize work.

Does this mean that we must throw away the lessons of research gained from studies of employee-centered supervision? No, it does not. It is doubtful that a new generation of managers would revert to the simple autocracy of an earlier epoch. What we are suggesting is not a return to an older type of management but a step up into a new kind. Much of the recent research on employee-centered supervision from the University of Michigan suggests that although employee-centered supervisors will have groups with high morale it is impossible to predict that such behavior will result in high productivity. In one recent study (46) the autocratic supervisor actually stimulated higher levels of output than the democratic supervisor.

In summary, what is the task of the supervisor? He will have to learn discriminatively to recognize good work, to reward this good work appropriately. This emphasis does not reduce the necessity for the maintenance of optimal personal relationships between supervisor and subordinate. In addition, he will have to acquire increasingly greater skills in the organization and distribution of work so that the possibility for successful achievement on the part of his subordinates will be increased. These reflections apply to supervisors on any level, from the foreman over a group of machinists to a company president dealing with his department heads.

What Then Becomes of the Concept of Participation?

The notion of participation is a loose one. It is clear, as several critics have recently suggested, that the authoritarian pattern of American industry will continue despite the propaganda for a more democratic way of life. This is inevitable, since in a large and complex institution true participation at every level in the setting of the goals for work is clearly impossible. The need for centralized management, for the coordination of one unit of an organization with another, is too great. More and more of our economy is being concentrated into large organizations.

Although there is no room for individual participation in the setting of goals, it is certainly possible that the ways in which these goals are to be reached can be left to the judgment of

individuals. Within certain limits, it is likely that more latitude
than is currently available to most people in industry can be given
to individuals to develop their own ways of achieving the ends
that are presented to them by a centralized authority. This is a
reasonable solution to the problem of motivation, more reasonable than the usual formulation of participation. To expect individuals at lower levels in an organization to exercise control
over the establishment of over-all goals is unrealistic. Thus,
when participation is suggested in these terms, it is usually a
sham.

A Program in Mental Health

There are some implications of this for the important issue of
mental health in industry. Most mental-health programs have
been focused on the solution of the problems of the mentally ill.
This is certainly not an area that can be neglected. The psychotic
must be found and treated. The neurotic should have expert
counseling.

Yet is this the most important aspect of the problem of mental
health? Note our findings. Only a very small proportion of the
individuals in our sample showed overt symptoms of a breakdown, even under severe conditions of stress. Undoubtedly this
minority needed clinical treatment. It is also true that to some
undetermined extent the elimination of poor hygienic conditions
might have prevented some of these breakdowns.

A more important aspect of our findings is the tone of the
reports of periods during which job attitudes were high. One
could almost say by definition that a period during which one's
attitudes toward one's work is strongly positive is a period of
good adjustment. Descriptions of improved interpersonal relationships, of increased ability to focus on work, and of an increased sense of confirmation of one's vocational goals all argue
a kind of value to positive attitudes toward the job that should be
the major end of a mental-health program in industry. This im-
plies that the one most significant thing to be done to raise the
mental health of the majority of our citizens is to increase the
potential for motivation in their work. Thus a program in mental
health becomes not an encapsulated and isolated attack on the

problem of the individual neurotic, the alcoholic, or the psychopath but a positive force for the entire community.

The Final Goal

The usual practice of industry is to search for a mode of operation that will yield the maximum of gain consistent with a minimum of risk. The prescriptions we have discussed in the preceding section, if they were carried out, would probably result in a greater degree of variability of individual output. Some people, given the chance to control their own work, would improve markedly; some would deteriorate to a certain extent, as they failed for reasons of personal adjustment or of skill to meet the challenge of freedom. It is likely, as the findings of this study would suggest, that the over-all level of the entire change would be upward. Our findings suggest that with an increase of motivation the freeing of creative push would undoubtedly lead to some remarkable advances on the part of those individuals capable of them.

However, supervisory and managerial people would be given the burden of a more difficult task of evaluation and of control than is true under a rigid and bureaucratic system. Instead of laying down rigid rules and demanding that these rules be followed, a supervisor would have to trust his ability to discriminate good end results from poor end results. The bureaucratic supervisor need not do so, since he usually assumes that the person he is supervising will follow out the predetermined steps and end with the usual dreary uniformity of the assigned product.

A further implication of greater variability in performance is that improvement in work would be more heavily rewarded than at present, both with direct recognition and with material rewards. Similarly, management would be given the burden of recognizing and reacting to poor performance.

As we have pointed out before, we realize that there are large segments of our society to which these prescriptions cannot possibly apply. It may be that for them the good life will have to come from fruitful hobbies and from improved lives outside the job. We would hope that as our society evolves this group would become smaller and smaller. Thus we reject the pessimism that views the future as one in which work will become increasingly meaningless to most people and in which the pursuits of leisure will become the most important end of our society. We cannot help but feel that the greatest fulfillment of man is to be found in activities that are meaningfully related to his own needs as well as those of society.

Appendix I

Job Attitudes
Patterned Interview

Think of a time when you felt exceptionally good or exceptionally bad about your job, either your present job or any other job you have had. This can be either the "long-range" or the "short-range" kind of situation, as I have just described it. Tell me what happened.

1. How long ago did this happen?
2. How long did the feeling last? Can you describe specifically what made the change of feelings begin? When did it end?
3. (For obviously SR sequences.) Was what happened typical of what was going on at the time?
4. Can you tell me more precisely why you felt the way you did at the time?
5. What did these events mean to you?
6. Did these feelings affect the way you did your job? How? How long did this go on?
7. Can you give me a specific example of the way in which your performance on the job was affected? (For productivity effects when the effect information was vague.) How long?
8. Did what happened affect you personally in any way? How long? Did it change the way you got along with people in general or your family? Did it affect your sleep, appetite, digestion, general health?
9. Did what happened basically affect the way you felt about working

at that company or did it merely make you feel good or bad about the occurrence itself?

10. Did the consequences of what happened at this time affect your career? How?

11. Did what happened change the way you felt about your profession? How?

12. How seriously were your feelings (good or bad) about your job affected by what happened? Pick a spot on the line below to indicate how strong you think the good or bad feelings were. Circle that position on the line.

Least									Average								Greatest			
1	2	3	4	5	6	7	8	9	10	11	12	13	14	15	16	17	18	19	20	21

Note: 1 should be used for a sequence that hardly affected your feelings at all; 21 should be used for a sequence that affected your feelings as seriously as the most important events in your working experience.

13. Could the situation you described happen again for the same reasons and with the same effects? If not, describe the changes that have taken place which would make your feelings and actions different today than they were then.

14. Is there anything else you would like to say about the sequence of events you have described?

What did you think of the interview?

Have you any other comments on the interview or on the research?

Notes:

For second sequence

Now that you described a time when you felt _____ about your job, please think of another time, one during which you felt exceptionally _____ about your job, preferably a _____ range sequence of events.

Appendix **II**

Analysis of Factors

1. Recognition—first level

   0. Not mentioned.
   1. Work praised—no reward.
   2. Work praised—reward given.
   3. Work noticed—no praise.
   4. Work not noticed.
   5. Good idea(s) not accepted.
   6. Inadequate work blamed or criticized—no punishment.
   7. Inadequate work blamed or criticized—punishment given.
   8. Successful work blamed or criticized—no punishment.
   9. Successful work blamed or criticized—punishment given.
   R. Credit for work taken by supervisor or other.
   X. Idea accepted by company.

2. Achievement—first level

   0. Not mentioned.
   1. Successful completion of job, or aspect of it.
   2. The having of a good idea—a solution to a problem.
   3. Made money for the company.
   4. Vindication—demonstration of rightness to doubters or challengers.
   5. Failure in job, or aspect of it.
   6. Seeing results of work.
   7. Not seeing results of work.

3. Possibility of growth—first level

   0. Not mentioned.
   1. Growth in skills—objective evidence.
   2. Growth in status (advancement)—objective evidence.
   3. Lack of opportunity for growth—objective evidence.

143

4. Advancement—first level

0. Not mentioned.
1. Received unexpected advancement.
2. Received advancement (expected or expectation not mentioned).
3. Failed to receive expected advancement.
4. Demotion.

5. Salary—first level

0. Not mentioned.
1. Received wage increase (expected or expectation not mentioned).
2. Received unexpected wage increase.
3. Did not receive expected increase.
4. Received wage increase less or later than expected.
5. Amount of salary.
6. Wages compare favorably with others doing similar or same job.
7. Wages compare unfavorably with others doing similar or same job.

6. Interpersonal relations—supervisor—first level

0. Not mentioned.
1. Friendly relations with supervisor.
2. Unfriendly relations with supervisor.
3. Learned a great deal from supervisor.
4. Supervisor went to bat for him with management.
5. Supervisor did not support him with management.
6. Supervisor honest.
7. Supervisor dishonest.
8. Supervisor willing to listen to suggestions.
9. Supervisor unwilling to listen to suggestions.
R. Supervisor gave credit for work done.
X. Supervisor withheld credit.

7. Interpersonal relations—subordinates—first level

0. Not mentioned.
1. Good working relationship with subordinates.
2. Poor working relationship with subordinates.
3. Good personal relationship with subordinates.
4. Poor personal relationship with subordinates.

8. Interpersonal relations—peers—first level

0. Not mentioned.
1. Liked people he worked with.

2. Did not like people he worked with.
3. Cooperation of people he worked with.
4. Lack of cooperation on the part of his co-workers.
5. Was part of a cohesive group.
6. Was isolated from group.

9. Supervision—technical—first level

0. Not mentioned.
1. Supervisor competent.
2. Supervisor incompetent.
3. Supervisor tried to do everything himself.
4. Supervisor delegated work well.
5. Supervisor consistently critical.
6. Supervisor showed favoritism.

10. Responsibility—first level

0. Not mentioned.
1. Allowed to work without supervision.
2. Responsible (for his own efforts).
3. Given responsibility for the work of others.
4. Lack of responsibility.
5. Given new responsibility—no formal advancement.

11. Company policy and administration—first level

0. Not mentioned.
1. Effective organization of work.
2. Harmful or ineffective organization of work.
3. Beneficial personnel policies.
4. Harmful personnel policies.
5. Agreement with company goals.
6. Disagreement with company goals.
7. High company status.
8. Low company status.

12. Working conditions—first level

0. Not mentioned.
1. Work isolated.
2. Work in social surroundings.
3. Good physical surroundings.
4. Poor physical surroundings.
5. Good facilities.
6. Poor facilities.
7. Right amount of work.
8. Too much work.
9. Too little work.

13. The work itself—first level

0. Not mentioned.
1. Routine.
2. Varied.
3. Creative (challenging).
4. Too easy.
5. Too difficult.
6. Opportunity to do a whole job—all phases.

14. Factors in personal life—first level

0. Not mentioned.
1. Family problems.
2. Community and other outside situations.
3. Family needs and aspirations salarywise.

15. Status—first level

0. Not mentioned.
1. Signs or appurtenances of status.
2. Having a given status.
3. Not having a given status.

16. Job security—first level

0. Not mentioned.
1. Tenure or other objective signs of job security.
2. Lack of objective signs of security (i.e., company instability).

17. Recognition—second level

0. Not mentioned.
1. First-level factors perceived as source of feelings of recognition.
2. First-level factors perceived as source of failure to obtain recognition.
3. First-level factors perceived as source of disapproval.

18. Achievement—second level

0. Not mentioned.
1. First-level factors perceived as source of achievement.
2. First-level factors perceived as source of failure.

19. Possible growth—second level

0. Not mentioned.
1. First-level factors perceived as leading to possible growth.
2. First-level factors perceived as block to growth.
3. First-level factors perceived as evidence of actual growth.

20. Advancement—second level

    0. Not mentioned.

    1. Feelings of advancement derived from changes in job situation.

    2. Feelings of demotion derived from changes in job situation.

21. Responsibility—second level

    0. Not mentioned.

    1. First-level factors leading to feelings of responsibility.

    2. First-level factors as source of feelings of lack of responsibility or diminished responsibility.

22. Group feeling—second level

    0. Not mentioned.

    1. Feelings of belonging—social.

    2. Feelings of isolation—social.

    3. Feelings of belonging—sociotechnical.

    4. Feelings of isolation—sociotechnical.

    5. Positive feelings toward group.

    6. Negative feelings toward group.

23. The work itself—second level

    0. Not mentioned.

    1. First-level factors leading to interest in performance of the job.

    2. First-level factors leading to lack of interest in performance of the job.

24. Status—second level

    0. Not mentioned.

    1. First-level factors as source of feelings of increased status.

    2. First-level factors as source of feelings of decreased status.

25. Security—second level

    0. Not mentioned.

    1. First-level factors as source of feelings of security.

    2. First-level factors as source of feelings of insecurity.

26. Feelings of fairness or unfairness—second level

    0. Not mentioned.

    1. First-level factor perceived as fair.

    2. First-level factor perceived as unfair.

    3. First-level factor perceived as source of feelings of disappointment in others.

27. Feelings of pride or shame

0. Not mentioned.
1. First-level factors as source of feelings of pride.
2. First-level factors as source of feelings of shame.
3. First-level factors as source of feelings of diminished pride.

28. Salary—second level

0. Not mentioned.
1. First-level factors perceived as source of ability to improve well-being.
2. First-level factors perceived as source of lack of ability to improve well-being.
3. First-level factors perceived as source of more money (need undetermined).
4. First-level factors perceived as source of lack of more money (need undetermined).

Analysis of Effects

1. Performance effects

0. Not mentioned.
1. General statements regarding positive change in quality or output of work.
2. General statements regarding negative change in quality or output of work.
3. Positive changes in rate or amount of time spent in work.
4. Negative changes in rate or amount of time spent in work.
5. Specific reports of positive changes in quality or nature of work.
6. Specific reports of negative changes in quality or nature of work.
7. Reports of positive changes in *both* rate and quality of work.
8. Reports of negative changes in *both* rate and quality of work.
9. Statement affirming lack of change in amount or quality of work.

2. Turnover effects

0. Not mentioned.
1. Quit.
2. Made connections.

3. Read papers—looked around—took steps but without contacting companies or agencies.
4. Thought of quitting.
5. No thought of quitting despite negative feelings.
6. Would not quit now because of positive feelings.
7. Would not quit despite specific offers.
8. Factor in decision to quit at later date.

3. Mental-health effects

0. Not mentioned.
1. Loss of sleep.
2. Psychosomatic effects.
3. Psychological effects of tension (anxiety, loss of appetite, headaches, etc.).
4. Psychosomatic effects and tension symptoms.
5. Improvement in psychosomatic conditions.
6. Improvement in tension symptoms.
7. Improvement in psychosomatic condition and tension symptoms.

4. Interpersonal relations effects

0. Not mentioned.
1. General statements regarding positive effects.
2. General statements regarding negative effects.
3. Positive effects on family.
4. Negative effects on family.
5. Positive effects on friends.
6. Negative effects on friends.
7. Positive effects on co-workers.
8. Negative effects on co-workers.
9. Many specific positive effects on interpersonal relations.
R. Many specific negative effects on interpersonal relations.

5. Attitudinal effects

0. Not mentioned.
1. Positive toward individual (supervisor).
2. Negative toward individual (supervisor).
3. Positive toward company.
4. Negative toward company.
5. Positive toward profession.
6. Negative toward profession.
7. Positive security feelings.
8. Negative security feelings.
9. Positive effects regarding confidence.

R. Negative effects regarding confidence.

X. Multiple effects on attitude (positive).

6. Miscellaneous effects

0. Not mentioned.

1. By products—effects of effects affecting other than job life.

2. Direct effects of attitudes affecting other than job life.

References

1. *Annual Review of Psychology.* Stanford, California: Stanford University Press, 1955.
2. Arendt, Hannah. *The human condition.* Chicago: University of Chicago Press, 1958.
3. Arensberg, C. M., and D. McGregor. Determination of morale in an industrial company. *Appl. Anthrop.*, 1942, 1 (2), 12–34.
4. Argyris, C. *Personality and organization; the conflict between system and the individual.* New York: Harper, 1957.
5. Bavelas, A. In D. Cartwright and A. Zander (eds.), *Group dynamics.* Evanston, Illinois: Row, Peterson, 1953.
6. Berelson, B. *Content analysis in communication research.* Glencoe, Illinois: Free Press, 1952.
7. Blum, F. A. *Toward a democratic work process.* New York: Harper, 1953.
8. Brayfield, A. H., and W. H. Crockett. Employee attitudes and employee performance. *Psychol. Bull.*, 1955 (52) 5, 396–424.
9. Brown, J. A. C. *The social psychology of industry.* London: Penguin Books, 1954.
10. Caplow, T., and R. McGee. *The academic marketplace.* New York: Basic Books, 1958.
11. Coch, L., and J. R. P. French. Overcoming resistance to change. *Hum. Relat.*, 1948, 1, 512–532.
12. Coombs, C. H. *A theory of psychological scaling.* Engineering Research Institute Bull. No. 34. Ann Arbor, Michigan: University of Michigan, 1951.
13. DeGrazia, S. *The political community.* Chicago: University of Chicago Press, 1950.
14. Dickson, W. J. The Hawthorne plan of personnel counseling. *Amer. Journ. of Ortho. Psychy.*, 1945, 15, 343–347.
15. Durkheim, E. *Suicide: a study in sociology.* Glencoe, Illinois: The Free Press, 1951.

151

16. Flanagan, J.   The critical incident technique.   *Psychol. Bull.*, 1954, 51, 327–358.

17. Fromm, E.   *The sane society.*   New York: Rinehart, 1955.

18. Green, B.   Attitude measurement in G. Lindzey (ed.).   *Handbook of social psychology.*   Cambridge, Massachusetts: Addison-Wesley, 1954.

19. Heron, Alastair.   The establishment for research purposes of two criteria of occupational adjustment.   *Occup. Psychol., Lond.*, 1952, 26, 78–85.

20. Hersey, R. B.   Emotional factors in accidents.   *Personnel J.*, 1936, 15, 59–65.

21. Herzberg, F.   An analysis of morale survey comments.   *Personnel Psychol.*, 1954, 7 (2), 267–275.

22. ———.   *Psychological Service Morale Surveys.*   Pittsburgh: Psychological Service of Pittsburgh, 1954.

23. ———, B. Mausner, R. Peterson, and D. Capwell.   *Job attitudes: Review of research and opinion.*   Pittsburgh: Psychological Service of Pittsburgh, 1957.

24. Homans, G. C.   *The human group.*   New York: Harcourt, Brace, 1950.

25. Hoppock, R.   *Job satisfaction.*   New York: Harper, 1935.

26. Horsfall, A. B., and C. M. Arensberg.   Teamwork and productivity in a shoe factory.   *Hum. Organization*, 1949, 8, 13–25.

27. Hughes, E. C.   The knitting of racial groups in industry.   *Amer. sociol. Rev.*, 1946, 11, 512–519.

28. Kahn, R. L.   The prediction of productivity.   *Journ. of Social Issues*, 1956, 12, 41–49.

29. Katz, D.   Morale and motivation in industry.   In Dennis, W. (ed.), *Current trends in industrial psychology.*   Pittsburgh: University of Pittsburgh Press, 1949, 145–171.

30. ———, and R. L. Kahn.   *Some recent findings in human relations research.*   Ann Arbor, Michigan: University of Michigan Survey Research Center, 1952.

31. Katz, D., N. Macoby, and N. Morse.   *Productivity, supervision and morale in an office situation.*   Part I.   Ann Arbor, Michigan: University of Michigan, Inst. for soc. Res., 1951.

32. Kerr, W.   Labor turn over and its correlates.   *J. appl. Psychol.*, 1947, 31, 366–371.

33. Lasswell, H. D.   *Language and politics.*   New York: E. W. Stewart, 1949.

34. Lazarsfeld, P. F. *The language of social research.* Glencoe, Illinois: Free Press, 1955.

35. Lewin, Kurt. *Resolving social conflict.* New York: Harper, 1950.

36. ———. *Field theory in social science.* New York: Harper, 1951.

37. Lincoln, J. F. *Lincoln's incentive system.* New York: McGraw-Hill, 1946.

38. Malinowski, B. *A scientific theory of culture and other essays.* Chapel Hill, North Carolina: University of North Carolina Press, 1944.

39. Mann, F., et al. *A comparison of high morale and low morale employees.* Unpublished study, 1949.

40. Maslow, A. H. A theory of motivation. *Psychol. Rev.,* 1943, 50, 370–396.

41. ———. *Motivation and personality.* New York: Harper, 1954.

42. Mayo, Elton. *The human problems of an industrial civilization.* New York: Macmillan, 1933.

43. McFarland, K. Why men and women get fired. *Personnel Journ.,* 1957, 35, 307–308.

44. McMurry, R. N. The case for benevolent autocracy. *Harv. Bus. Rev.,* 1958, 36 (5), 82–90.

45. Merton, R. K., et al. *The focused interview.* Glencoe, Illinois: Free Press, 1955.

46. Morse, N., and E. Reimer. The experimental change of a major organizational variable. *J. abnorm. soc. Psychol.,* 1956, 52, 120–129.

47. Packard, Vance. *The hidden persuaders.* New York: McKay, 1957.

48. Pfiffner, J. M. The effective supervisor: an organization research study. *Personnel,* 1955, 31, 530–540.

49. Purcell, T. *The worker speaks his mind on company and union.* Cambridge, Massachusetts: Harvard University Press, 1953.

50. ———. Dual allegiance to company and union—packinghouse workers. *Personnel Psychol.,* 1954, 7, 48–58.

51. Roethlisberger, F. J., and W. J. Dickson. *Management and the worker.* Cambridge, Massachusetts: Harvard University Press, 1947.

52. Seashore, Stanley E. *Group cohesiveness in the industrial work group.* Ann Arbor, Michigan: University of Michigan, Survey Research Center, 1954.

53. S. R. A. *Employee inventory.* Chicago: Science Research Associates, 1951.

54. Stagner, R.   Psychological aspects of industrial conflict: I. Perception. *Personnel Psychol.*, 1948, 1, 131–143.
55. Stockford, L., and K. Kunze.   Psychology and the pay check. *Personnel*, 1950, 27, 129–143.
56. Walker, C. R.   *Steeltown.*   New York: Harper, 1950.
57. ———.   *Toward the automatic factory:* a case study of men and machines.   New Haven: Yale University Press, 1957.
58. Whyte, W. F.   *Money and motivation.*   New York: Harper, 1955.
59. Whyte, W. H., Jr.   *The organization man.*   New York: Simon and Schuster, 1956.
60. Wickert, F.   Turnover, and employees' feelings of ego-involvement in the day-to-day operations of a company.   *Personnel Psychol.*, 1951, 4, 185–197.
61. Zaleznik, A.   *Worker satisfaction and development.*   Boston: Division of Research, Harvard Business School, 1956.

Index